Presented to

I AM
THE
VISION

I AM THE VISION

How Deep Ownership Propels Exceptional
Performance and Rapid Advancement

TIFFANY FARLEY

Miracle Word
Publishing

Published in Virginia Beach, Virginia by Miracle Word Publishing.

Scripture quotations taken from the Amplified® Bible (AMP), Copyright © 2015 by The Lockman Foundation. Used by permission. (www.lockman.org)

Scripture quotations are from the ESV® Bible (The Holy Bible, English Standard Version®), copyright © 2001 by Crossway, a publishing ministry of Good News Publishers. Used by permission. All rights reserved.

The Scriptures quoted from the NET Bible® https://netbible.com copyright ©1996, 2019 used with permission from Biblical Studies Press, L.L.C. All rights reserved.

Scripture taken from the New King James Version®. Copyright © 1982 by Thomas Nelson. Used by permission. All rights reserved.

Scripture quotations marked (NLT) are taken from the Holy Bible, New Living Translation, copyright ©1996, 2004, 2015 by Tyndale House Foundation. Used by permission of Tyndale House Publishers, Carol Stream, Illinois 60188. All rights reserved.

All uppercase and italicized text in verses of Scripture are added by the author for the purpose of emphasis.

ISBN 978-1-7349962-9-6

Printed in the United States of America

To the Miracle Word Team, present & future.
Divine possession is for the faithful.

. . . and that's us.

CONTENTS

FOREWORD

I was in the middle of preaching my message during one night of a revival in Indiana when I heard a noise behind me.

I turned around, and to my surprise, a man was standing on the far side of the sanctuary wearing jeans, boots, and a brown Carhartt jacket. He had an acoustic guitar strapped on and was strumming it loudly—everything was not okay.

"Put that guitar down and take a seat!" I shouted from the other side of the church.

"I'm God!" came the booming reply.

So we're dealing with a demon, I thought. I felt the gift of faith stirring inside me as I stalked across the church with fire in my eyes.

The pastor had accidentally left the door at the altar unlocked. It opened directly to the parking lot, and this demonized man had wandered in from the street . . . with his guitar.

Seconds later, I stood nose-to-nose with him until our foreheads almost touched. He quickly retreated until his back was against the wall. He must have seen that fire in my eyes because he managed to squeak, "God bless you," in a very small voice.

By the authority of the Holy Spirit, I took control and handled the situation, but not without irritation.

Where the heck were the ushers? What if that man had come in with a gun or a knife?

Big dropped ball.

I later discovered that the ushers did know what was happening . . . they just didn't care enough to take action.

As soon as the demonized man walked in, Zack, one of my team members, approached the head usher, who was standing in the back of the sanctuary leaning against the wall.

"Do you have any idea who this guy is or what he's doing?" Zack asked. The usher leaned forward slightly and glanced at the demonized man.

"Huh. Nope. Never seen him before in my life," he replied and leaned back with one foot against the wall.

The head usher held a title, but he was useless. He was the opposite of invaluable to the vision; he was disposable. Fully and utterly replaceable.

But what if that usher had been the one preaching? I guarantee you he wouldn't have wanted a demon-possessed vagrant interrupting his message. He would have wanted someone to maintain order in the service.

That usher didn't see himself as part of the vision. He was just there. Holding a title, filling a role—but not taking ownership. And the truth is, people like that are easy to spot. They're indifferent. They don't take initiative. They don't care about the big picture because they don't see themselves in it. They punch the clock, do the bare minimum, and leave. You can count on them to do exactly what's required—and not one bit more.

But what if he had owned the vision? What if he had treated that service as his own? I guarantee you, he wouldn't have leaned back against the wall like a spectator. He would have leapt into action, making sure that nothing disrupted the flow of what God was doing in that service. He would have defended the atmosphere and made excellence his priority because that's what vision-driven people do.

That's exactly what this book, *I Am the Vision*, is about: taking full ownership of the vision you're serving. It's about seeing yourself as more than just an employee, volunteer, or team member—it's about becoming the vision. When you treat the organization or mission you're part of as if it were your own, everything changes. Excellence becomes your standard, and results start to follow.

When you "become the vision," something powerful

happens. Your work stops being ordinary. People notice. Excellence always provokes promotion. In Proverbs 22:29, the Bible says, "Do you see a man skillful in his work? He will stand before kings; he will not stand before obscure men." That's a promise for anyone willing to embrace this mindset. When you stop thinking like an employee and start thinking like an owner, you make yourself invaluable to the organization.

This book will challenge you. It will push you to think differently about the role you play, the way you approach your tasks, and the way you view the vision to which you're connected. It's not just about showing up—it's about stepping up.

The rewards for adopting this mindset are enormous. You'll find that doors of opportunity swing open for you. People will start trusting you with more, promoting you, and recognizing the value you bring to the table. You'll cultivate the kind of reputation that can't be bought—a reputation for excellence, dependability, and leadership. And even better, you'll find fulfillment in knowing that you've given your best to something bigger than yourself.

Tiffany has done this for our ministry, and that's why she's perfectly suited to write this book. I've never had to wonder if her work would be excellent or if it would be completed on time. She treats every responsibility as though she leads the organization—with a desire to see the ideal results any owner would celebrate.

If you're ready to stop going through the motions and start standing out—if you're ready to align yourself fully with the vision and take ownership—then this book is for you. Tiffany's insights and principles will show you exactly how to do it, and I promise you this: If you apply what you read, you won't stay where you are for long.

Get ready to shift. Get ready to grow. Get ready to become the vision.

Pastor Ted Shuttlesworth Jr.
Miracle Word Church
West Palm Beach, FL

INTRODUCTION

But the path of the righteous is like the light of dawn, which shines brighter and brighter until full day.

Proverbs 4:18 ESV

To be invaluable. It means "valuable beyond estimation." It describes something or someone whose worth is so profound that it cannot be quantified or assigned a price. That's exactly the level of contribution I want to bring to my team and what I look for in those who join me.

Being an invaluable asset to your team reflects your skills, expertise, reliability, attitude, problem-solving abilities, and versatility. It means you contribute such significant value that it defies measurement, strengthening the team in ways beyond any single description.

But what makes you invaluable? What is it that truly sets you apart? How do you build a team that is so valuable no one can adequately describe it?

Seth Godin, a renowned author, entrepreneur, and, as many would argue, a marketing genius, wrote a book titled *Linchpin: Are You Indispensable?* In this book, he teaches the importance of a linchpin within the mechanical workings of something like a wheel. Though small and seemingly insignificant, a wheel quickly falls off its axle if this pin is not in its proper place and function.[1]

The linchpin carries a role of great value. Though not often visible on the outside, its strength holds everything together.

In the same way, an organization, a team, or even a vision without a linchpin is at risk of falling apart. Godin describes a linchpin as an indispensable element, someone who is deeply engaged, emotionally invested, and relentlessly dedicated to driving a vision forward.[2]

Linchpins choose to take ownership. They commit wholeheartedly and show up consistently, even in the face of challenges. It's about caring so deeply for the vision that it becomes an inseparable part of who you are.

When you take ownership, you do what's beyond your paycheck, and the long-term result is trust, influence, and indispensability. Leaders and team members will come to see you as *essential* instead of optional, leading to greater opportunities, promotions, and rewards—because your value becomes undeniable.

This level of ownership will elevate not only your own performance but the entire mission of your team. It is far more than just fulfilling a role—it's about becoming a vital force. This identity shift allows you to unlock a power that propels you far beyond ordinary achievement.

Having a vision can change your whole life. Just ask Abraham. When you understand your purpose and what God said you can have, you won't be satisfied with anything less.

You have greatness on the inside of you. You are not called to be mediocre. But success is never automatic. It requires taking action and unwavering diligence.

This book will help you whether you're part of a team or leading one. It will show you how to cultivate an unshakable commitment to your vision and the God-given purpose that fuels it.

I am not a perfect team member, and I do not have it all figured out. Not a day passes without reminding me how imperative each of the lessons in this book truly are.

Somewhere along the way, I simply discovered something profound: The vision is no longer what I do but who I am.

I am the vision.

"For I am about to do something new.
See, I have already begun! Do you not see it?"

Isaiah 43:19 NLT

CHAPTER 01

THE GREAT PURSUIT

At the young age of seventeen, a boy was dying. Months had passed as he lay a prisoner in his own bed, bleeding from deep inside his lungs.

In those days, tuberculosis was a death sentence—and his was being written. One night, it looked like the worst had finally come, and there was nothing more doctors could do. His family gathered around his bed preparing for him to die, and his mother wept bitterly.

Later that night, the boy saw a vision. On one side of his bed, he saw his coffin, and on the other, a large open Bible reaching floor to ceiling. As he looked at each, God asked him to choose.

He said, "Which one of these will you choose tonight?" It wasn't an audible voice but as firm and sure as any voice he had ever heard. He knew the coffin would mean his death, but the Bible was a call to preach.[1]

Despite his hesitation, being caught between two

things he desperately didn't want to do, the boy answered the call of God and chose to preach the gospel so he could live. He fell asleep with an unwavering commitment to fulfill his choice. A miracle took place, and the Lord healed his body that night.[2]

That boy was Lester Sumrall, a world-renowned pastor and evangelist. From that sickbed, he went on to preach the gospel and serve the Lord for sixty-five years. He ministered in 110 countries and authored more than 130 books. He founded LeSEA, Lester Sumrall Evangelistic Association, which birthed multiple television and radio stations, a satellite ministry, and much more.[3]

By the time Lester Sumrall reached the final years of his life, he had accomplished more than most Christian ministries ever will. Even then, his vision did not dim with age.

One night in Denver, he received a prophetic word that God would soon ask him to launch a new area of ministry larger than anything he had ever done. *And he did.*

Lester Sumrall later admitted in his autobiography that he had seen himself building more television stations, but God had something even greater. One of the things that you will quickly learn as a child of God is that he always has bigger ideas than you. Even when you *think* you're already thinking big.

While he was visiting Jerusalem, God told him that his people were dying of starvation and needed to be fed, not just with bread, but that providing the food would be a miracle in their eyes. God warned him that famine would come in the end times. Lester Sumrall understood that providing food to starving people worldwide would be a direct opportunity to share the gospel.

For the next five hours, God gave him specific instructions that night on how to accomplish this vision. This story is a powerful example of how God will not only show you *what* you are to do but also lead you in *how* to do it. He knows how to do things the best way every time.

God instructed him to bring food quickly to many places by airplane due to the heavy corruption. Attempting to provide relief aid to many countries can be frustrating and often a wasted effort when corrupt officials steal the supplies at the ship dock or impose exorbitant "import fees." The infrastructure to properly deliver food and supplies in many areas simply did not exist.

He repeatedly heard one word in his spirit that didn't bring immediate understanding at the time—*Hercules*. Lester Sumrall returned to South Bend, Indiana, and began sharing this brand-new vision with his team.

After communicating the undeniable need to do this by aircraft, he turned to his ministry pilot, Thorpe Mitchell, and asked him what a "Hercules" was.

His pilot informed him that Hercules was the name

for a Lockheed C-130, primarily a military aircraft. No other airliner could take food into the primitive areas of the world as successfully. This specific instruction from the Lord was what they needed to carry out the vision.

God does not ignore the details. Sumrall's ministry pilot had spent much of his earlier career in the United States military command. He knew the supervisor of the Lockheed C-130 Hercules program. This aircraft would cost $30 million brand new, so they decided to look at previously used options.

They soon located an immaculate model that checked every box. They negotiated the price to an incredible $1.5 million. While it was still a significant amount of money to raise, it was much less than $30 million!

Once they had the money to buy it, the second obstacle was acquiring permission. The United States Department of State had to approve the sale of any modern in-use military aircraft.

The Federal Aviation Administration, which governs all civilian air matters in the United States, also had to allow it.[4]

Whenever I hear this story about Lester Sumrall acquiring a military aircraft to feed starving people in so many nations, I am in awe of every miracle God performed to make it happen. The testimony is intricately woven with such supernatural provision and favor.

Sumrall secured the necessary permissions—against all natural understanding. Just as the request was about to be denied, someone brought it directly to the President's attention.

The money came in, despite people insisting he would never afford an aircraft like that.

Lester Sumrall later recounted seeing his Hercules aircraft in front of their hangar at the airport and how his heart was full of joy. "I obeyed, and God provided. And I don't think there's any end to this vision."[5]

At the age of seventy-four, Lester Sumrall founded Feed The Hungry. When you read any of the last books he authored, he will ask you to catch this vision of feeding hungry people worldwide as one of God's final instructions for his life. And he was right. *The vision didn't end.*

At the time of writing this book, Feed The Hungry has provided over 100 million meals worldwide, and they feed 500,000 children daily.[6] They provide educational programs and share the gospel with the provision of these miracle meals—just as God instructed. He attached himself to this vision from the Lord and pursued it for the remainder of his life.

Lester Sumrall's obedience still makes a significant kingdom impact far beyond his time because vision doesn't die. People are still reading his books. People still talk about his faithfulness in pursuing his God-given vision.

What about you? Do you have a vision for your life? Are you living each day with purpose and design? Better yet, let's start at the beginning: Do you know what having a vision means and how to get one?

What Is Vision?

The importance of vision needs no introduction. You would be hard-pressed to discover any leadership book that doesn't talk about vision in some way.

In the context of purpose, vision means to see ahead. It is seeing God's divine plan unfold ahead of you. It is seeing a reality that does not yet exist. As I have often heard Bishop Rick Thomas, author of *Capturing the Mind of God*, say, "It is when God himself paints on the canvas of your mind."

Vision makes ordinary men extraordinary. Without it, what do you have?

The Bible says in Proverbs 29:18, "Where there is no prophetic vision the people cast off restraint." Scholars say this phrase "cast off restraint" can be seen as an example in Exodus 32:25, where it says, "Moses saw that the people were *running wild*, for Aaron had let them get completely out of control" (NET).[7]

In other words, there is chaos when there is no prophetic vision. People run wild when they have no divine direction. There is no order and no progress. Vision allows you to see where you are going. It gives you a measure to use daily to know your efforts are going in the right direction.

You may be skilled beyond the average person. However, skills used without aim and focus are wasteful. A lawyer does not invest years of their life and pay hundreds of thousands of dollars for a law degree they have no intention of using. Doctors do not learn how the human body intricately works together, only to graduate medical school with no desire to ever use their degree.

No, even before they enroll as students, they see themselves as future doctors and lawyers. They see themselves making a significant difference in society and saving lives. They have a clear vision and make it their target.

Imagine you are an Olympic runner. Your feet wear the very best sneakers money can buy. You've highly conditioned your body. You are ready to run with strength and speed at any given time. You were born to run.

But imagine you step out an unfamiliar door. The location is unknown to you, and you are wearing a blindfold. Not only has no one told you which direction you should go, but you cannot see correctly to determine your path.

Despite your athletic capability and extensive training, what you require most to run your race is nonexistent. *How are you expected to run if you cannot see?*

You may run in circles until you trip and fall. You may run straight into a wall, a tree, or even a busy traffic street. You would reach no desirable destination, and your experience would be painful and frustrating.

Imagine, then, if you were not alone. What if others around you were also trying to run the same way? Every direction, even if by chance it were the right one, would feel chaotic and even dangerous beyond measure.

Hard truth: If what you are leading is in chaos, it's because there is no vision or you have failed to communicate it. A lack of vision creates disorder and confusion. Whether personally or as a leader, vision is necessary to move from where you are to a new place.

You cannot properly lead people without telling them where you are going, and to follow someone who either doesn't know the desired destination or refuses to share it with you is crippling.

In the corporate world, businesses often have ten-year plans. Their vision statement is everywhere. They know where they are going. They've identified their desired outcome and the steps necessary to achieve it. They know what they must accomplish today to be closer to it tomorrow.

Unfortunately, in the church, many do not even have a plan for today, let alone years from now. Secular corporations are planning decades ahead, while many Christians wake up each day with zero intention of how they will spend it.

You must have a vision. You must seek the Lord to know his purpose for your life. After all, you are designed to see it. Vision is one of your most powerful assets because, as you read earlier in this chapter, ideas do not die.

Condemned as a heretic in 1536, an English priest named William Tyndale had a vision. A master of seven different languages, Tyndale was reading a Greek edition of the New Testament when he discovered the doctrine of justification by faith.[8]

During this era, the English Catholic Church taught that salvation was achieved through good works, meaning people must work their way to God. In addition to these good works and keeping the commandments, this would include participation in the sacraments, indulgences, penance, and other traditions of the Catholic Church. Since ordinary people could not read the Bible in its original languages, how could they know anything different?

Being saved by faith was a new revelation that would catapult the Protestant Reformation through leaders like Martin Luther and others, changing the course of church history forever.

Tyndale felt compelled to share this good news of justification by faith, and it became his life's passion. His vision was to create an English translation of the Bible that could be printed and made affordable for distribution so that ordinary men could read it.[9] He felt that everyone deserved to read God's Word in their language. There was just one small problem—it was illegal.

To control the circulation of teaching deemed heretical by the Catholic Church, a law was established that made it a crime punishable by death to translate the Bible into the common language.

Furthermore, it was illegal to even read the Bible in English. Once, church leaders burnt seven people at the stake—six men and one woman—for teaching their children the Ten Commandments, the Apostles' Creed, and the Lord's Prayer in English.[10] Even then, Tyndale's courage remained fueled as he refused to stop his efforts.

In 1526, William Tyndale translated and published the first-ever mechanically-printed New Testament in English.[11] The government desperately wanted to eliminate these English translations, so they spent a significant amount of money buying copies to burn and destroy. Ironically, the funds spent doing so made it back to the hands of Tyndale so he could continue his work.[12]

Not long after, William Tyndale was arrested and given a death sentence for what he believed. However, his translations would later become decisive in the very history of the English Bible that we know today.[13] You and I have access to the Word of God in a language we understand because of this man's vision. It was an idea that did not die with him but continued making an impact far beyond his life.

When you have a vision, you have a purpose. You are no longer living without an aim or target. In truth, you are no longer living for yourself when you have a vision. The impact of your single life begins to expand. It will no longer be just about you. Life becomes something greater.

Vision establishes your confidence because you know where you are going and what you will do when you get there. But what is a vision if not pursued? Knowing and seeing the vision clearly in your heart and mind is not enough. It is only the beginning.

Diligent Pursuit

Bishop David Oyedepo, pastor of the largest church in the world located in Ota, Nigeria, teaches on vision by recalling Newton's first law of motion. This law states that all things remain in a state of rest until a force of motion is applied.[14]

Your vision will remain at rest until you diligently pursue it. It will only ever be something you saw and never something you did.

If, as an Olympic runner, you see your destination and do not make every effort to run toward it, how do you expect to get there? Seeing your destination in itself does not produce arrival. When God gives you a vision for your life, you must diligently pursue it!

> *The sluggard does not plow in the autumn;*
> *he will seek at harvest and have nothing.*
> *Proverbs 20:4 ESV*

This proverb is a concept farmers know very well. They may look at their plot of land and envision fields of bountiful crops they will harvest. However, a farmer knows the crops will not just appear because they have a vision for it. Just as his harvest will only come with plowing and planting, your vision will only be attainable with a diligent pursuit.

Many mistake knowing their vision for pursuing it. They ignorantly wait on God to make it all happen, as if they are only along for the ride. But you see, God is not just a God of promises; he is a God of covenant. The two are not synonymous.

A promise indicates that one person assumes an active role while the other remains passive. If I were to make you a promise that I would wash the dishes, you would be confident that I would. Nothing about my promise requires you to do anything. You would simply enjoy the result of washed dishes.

However, if I say instead, I will wash the dishes if you

help me dry them, you can now see that both parties have an active role of obligation to fulfill.

Throughout Scripture, we can see how God makes a covenant with his people. God never just says he will bless you, nor does he promise to increase you no matter what. God requires action from you. If you do your part, which he has already equipped you to do, he will never fail to do his.

> *And if you faithfully obey the voice of the LORD your God, being careful to do all his commandments that I command you today, the LORD your God will set you high above all the nations of the earth. And all these blessings shall come upon you and overtake you, if you obey the voice of the LORD your God.*
>
> *Deuteronomy 28:1–2 ESV*

Notice how the great blessings promised here in Deuteronomy are conditional upon faithful obedience. In fact, the condition "if" is stated here not just once but twice!

> *But the steadfast love of the LORD is from everlasting to everlasting on those who fear him, and his righteousness to chil-*

dren's children, to those who keep his cov-
enant and remember to do his command-
ments.

Psalm 103:17–18 ESV

David writes that the Lord's steadfast love and righteousness are for those who fear him, keep his covenant,
and remember to keep his commandments. Those blessings are not just made available by default. Faithful obedience and a correct position of heart are the keys to receiving such promises from the Lord.

Come to me, all who labor and are heavy
laden, and I will give you rest. Take my
yoke upon you, and learn from me, for I
am gentle and lowly in heart, and you
will find rest for your souls.

Matthew 11:28–29 ESV

He even promises us rest with specific instructions
on receiving it. He does not promise us rest if we are
out there doing our own thing. He says we will find rest
when we come to him, exchange our earthly burdens for
his, and learn from him.

When God told Abram (later called Abraham) that he
would make him a great nation in Genesis 12, he was re-

quired to follow multiple steps of obedience. These actions of great faith didn't always make sense in the natural.

Abram did not passively wait for God to produce his destiny. Abram faithfully obeyed the Lord's instructions as he pursued the vision.

Likewise, God told the Israelites that the land of Canaan belonged to them. This land was their divine possession, but they didn't snap their fingers and find themselves living there. God required a diligent and obedient pursuit of what was already theirs to take. This truth is repeated throughout Scripture.

Can you see how you have a part in obtaining what God has for you? Nothing will feel as potentially "life-changing" as knowing your specific purpose. Finding your place in the body of Christ and knowing that you are carrying out God's plan for you is indescribably rewarding.

It's time to not only see it but to run toward it. Never let that vision go; never let anyone talk you out of it. Keep that vision in front of you at all times, and attach yourself to it with your whole heart.

"If you want to build a ship, don't drum up the people to gather wood, divide the work, and give orders. Instead, teach them to yearn for the vast endless sea."

Antoine de Saint-Exupéry

CHAPTER 02

TAKING OWNERSHIP

It is impossible to know the sport of tennis without recognizing the names Venus and Serena Williams. They are two of the greatest players in history.

Richard Williams had a dream for his daughters even before they were born. While watching a match featuring Virginia Ruzici, the 1978 French Open champion, he learned that she had earned $40,000 in just one week of tournament play—exceeding his entire annual income.

Curiosity drove him to buy a newspaper the following morning to verify Ruzici's earnings. He wanted to know whether tennis players could genuinely earn so much so quickly for what he described as "just hitting a tennis ball."

When he found out it was true, he returned home and told his wife, "We should have two more children and transform them into tennis superstars."

Richard had a vision for his daughters and his family.

He ordered instructional books and videos and taught himself the game. From a young age, he coached his daughters and ensured they had the skills and knowledge to excel at the sport.

Serena recalls in her memoir, "I just remember playing tennis all the time ... It was always there ... like breathing."[1]

But Richard knew that with all the coaching in the world, they wouldn't be great unless they decided to be. They needed athletic ability, yes. They required practice and skill, yes. But he also knew they needed a passion for the game and an iron will to succeed.

Though it started as a father's vision, somewhere along the way, his girls had to decide to take ownership and really want it for themselves. After all, you don't practice a sport for three to four hours per day, seven days a week, if you're just doing it for someone else.

Serena recalls her father telling her, "Whatever you become, you become in your head first."[2] She was taught to visualize who she would become until it became part of her, to see herself as the very best.

Venus has won seven Grand Slam singles titles, while her sister Serena, considered one of the greatest tennis players of all time, has won twenty-three.[3]

They took ownership of the vision until it became who they are ... *champions.*

Who You Are

Vision can make you an unstoppable force. Pursuing a vision with dedicated diligence will quickly set you apart in a world that too often settles for the mediocre and bare minimum. Taking ownership of the vision is the ultimate deciding factor of success because we greatly value what belongs to us.

There are many characteristics that define someone who works with excellence, and we will cover many of them in the chapters to come. But if you don't decide to take ownership, you'll never fully care about the vision deeply enough to do what it takes to make it happen.

A well-known story tells of a seasoned carpenter who was ready to retire. As he shared his plans with his employer, the boss made one final request: to build one last house. Though reluctant, the carpenter agreed to take on this final project.

However, the carpenter found himself cutting corners on the job. He didn't put in the same level of effort and attention to detail as he had with his previous contracts. He rushed through the construction so he could finally enjoy his retirement.

The carpenter finished the house and handed the keys to his boss, relieved he could now retire. His boss smiled and handed the keys right back. "We wanted to give you a retirement gift for helping us all these years. This last house I asked you to build is actually for you."

You can imagine the carpenter's face. If he had known the house he was building was his all along, he would have done so many things differently!

If he had known the materials purchased and the details that he could have included would all be his to enjoy, he would never have rushed through and done such a minimal job. He would have treated the project with deeper attention and care.

You will never value something that belongs to someone else the same way you would if it were yours. That is the power of owning the vision. It's a decision to move beyond the duty of the 9–5 because visionaries don't punch the clock.

Going beyond doesn't mean you work all day, every day. It means that even if you're serving someone else's vision, such as in ministry, you treat the vision like your own.

It's not the pastor's church. It's your church. Those aren't the ministry partners. They are your partners. It's not the ministry's website. It's your website. And because it's yours, it matters more.

I am talking about the very title of this book. *An ownership so deep that it becomes who you are.*

A Team in Sync

Sync is when two or more people or things move together in perfect unison, matching both timing and pace. I do not want to be on a team of people trying to all go in a different direction. It's imperative to be in sync with each other and our leadership for what God has called us to do.

When I think of a team moving and working in total sync, I think of military units. No matter the differing rank or position, each individual in any military team is focused on one thing—completing their mission.

Within a military team, there is an extreme level of trust, as often, their very survival depends on each other. They rigorously train for the mission at hand, and when in the field, no one treats the mission casually—quite the opposite. They are willing to give their lives and do whatever it takes.

When you know where God has called you, choose to be all in. God did not call me where I am to have me look elsewhere. Be a man of purpose. Be a woman of purpose. Know where you belong and fully identify with it.

When my leadership receives instruction from the Lord, I embrace it as my own, having already committed to seeing what they see. To serve the vision effectively, I must take complete ownership of it.

I understand that God has purposed me to be where I am, so if that's what leadership sees, that's what I see. If that's where leadership is going, that's where I'm going. If this is what God has asked them to build, then get me a hammer because we are building it together.

Ship Builders

We were in a week of revival in Lancaster, Pennsylvania, and the Holy Spirit moved so powerfully one night. My pastor was ministering and called the pastor of that church forward to give him a word from the Lord.

I was at the altar with my camera, photographing the night of ministry, which gave me a full view of what was happening. That night, I saw something that confirmed what I already knew about taking ownership of the vision.

As this Pennsylvania pastor began to receive his word from the Lord, members of his team started to raise their hands right where they were across the sanctuary. The Lord began to tell him of the soon-coming increase to his ministry and the big doors about to open for him.

But his team knew, "That's not just for my pastor; that's for me. *That's for us.* Where he is going, we are going. His increase is our increase." Each member of his team received that word personally.

As a leader, you can be a taskmaster, or you can invite your team to go where God is taking you. Showing your team the vision will give them what they need to run. It allows them to see what you see and commit to doing whatever it takes to accomplish it.

In his best-selling business book *Start with Why: How Great Leaders Inspire Everyone to Take Action*, Simon Sinek argues that "why" you do what you do is the most important element of your business structure, even more so than "what" you do, or "how" you do it.[4]

Building a team culture that effectively communicates and reinforces your "why" is the first step to inviting sailors to "yearn for the vast endless sea."

A sailor who finds their identity out on the water doesn't need coercing to build a ship to sail. If the sea is where they belong, determining how to get there will be their focus. You don't ever have to beg a sailor to sail. It's who they are.

A vision cannot remain unseen. You won't know how to get there if you can't see it. As author Zig Ziglar famously said, "You can't hit a target you cannot see, and you cannot see a target you do not have."[5]

As mentioned in the previous chapter, you cannot properly lead people without telling them where you are going. When you refuse to share the vision with your team in a clear way that makes taking ownership possible, you are crippling their potential to perform at their most effective capacity.

There's a stark difference between a team that mundanely executes a minimum number of tasks so they can be done with work for the day and a team that goes the extra mile at every opportunity because they know and understand their work directly impacts the bigger picture.

The Choice to Make

One of my earlier jobs following college was working during the day as an office administrator at a private medical office. As an employee, they expected me to represent the office professionally with the patients and their families.

There was an expectation in how I dressed, spoke with patients, and kept our front desk area organized and tidy. When I came to work each morning, that office and his patients were my focus. I was an integral part of his practice.

However, I never went home and began brainstorming about getting him more patients. I never found myself looking for books I could read to improve my medical knowledge or browsing the web looking for the latest medical office softwares we could implement.

When I left each day, I did not care about that office. Truthfully, I didn't care much when I was in that office either. I was there only to do a job—to clock in and clock out—and expected a paycheck for the hours I worked waiting on my desk every Friday.

Taking ownership is a choice. When you find your place and your purpose, it will be the easiest thing you ever decide to do. As a leader, don't you desire a team that runs alongside you?

When team members are genuinely invested and truly own the vision, they will be innovative, proactive, and loyally committed. The vision is no longer what they do but who they are.

"Distorted thoughts create distorted vision. It doesn't take numerous thoughts to throw your life off course, it takes just one."

Pastor Nancy Dufresne

CHAPTER 03

THE POSITION OF YOUR HEART

In 1 Kings 17, the Bible tells us the story of the prophet Elijah and the widow in Zarephath. Elijah had just prophesied to Ahab—the ruling king of Israel—that a three-year drought would hit the nation.

This event was significant because King Ahab worshiped Baal, who was believed by many to be the god of rain and abundant harvest. God was again showing the nation of Israel that he was the only true and living God and demonstrating his power and authority.

You think you're serving the god of rain? We'll see about that.

This made King Ahab angry. The Lord instructed Elijah to hide by Kerith Brook, where ravens would feed him.

Soon after, when the ongoing drought dried up the brook, God told Elijah to go to Zarephath, where a widow would care for him. God was proving that he could provide for whomever and however he pleased under any circumstance.

Widows were common during this period of history, filled with war and disease. However, unlike modern times, widows had no inheritance rights in those days. They often had to depend on charity for survival.

Elijah found her gathering sticks at the city gate. As this was a heavily trafficked area, the widow would have known this was a good place to search for anything that may have fallen off an entering load.

People typically offered various acts of hospitality to travelers at the city gate, but during drought and famine, someone like this widow would be focused on survival.

The conversation between Elijah and this widow of Zarephath is interesting to me.

> *So he arose and went to Zarephath. And when he came to the gate of the city, behold, a widow was there gathering sticks. And he called to her and said, "Bring me a little water in a vessel, that I may drink." And as she was going to bring it, he called to her and said, "Bring me a morsel of bread in your hand." And she said, "As the LORD your God lives, I have nothing baked, only a handful of flour in a jar and a little oil in*

a jug. And now I am gathering a couple of sticks that I may go in and prepare it for myself and my son, that we may eat it and die." And Elijah said to her, "Do not fear; go and do as you have said. But first make me a little cake of it and bring it to me, and afterward make something for yourself and your son.

1 Kings 17:10–13 ESV

Imagine being this widow. You are gathering twigs for a fire to cook the last meal you and your son will ever eat. You are preparing your final meal on this earth.

Trying to survive as a widow in times like these was already challenging enough, but it was even more difficult during a famine. Then, on this day, a prophet shows up and asks you for something that feels impossible and appears to lack compassion and understanding.

Here she is, trying to find enough sticks so she and her son can eat their final meal before starving to death, and Elijah barely seems to care about her situation.

She's probably experiencing what I imagine to be the most hopeless and devastating day of her life. After telling the prophet about her horrible reality, he tells her to continue with this exact plan, but first, to make him some bread.

Earlier in verse 9, we read that God tells Elijah that he has already told the widow to provide for him. The passage doesn't reveal anything further about whether he told her any details or her initial response, but it does tell us that this widow knew it was her responsibility to take care of the prophet.

Of course, we know how miraculous the story turned out. Read on, and you'll find that the widow's flour and oil never ran out during the remainder of the drought.

> For thus says the LORD, the God of Israel, "The jar of flour shall not be spent, and the jug of oil shall not be empty, until the day that the LORD sends rain upon the earth." And she went and did as Elijah said. And she and he and her household ate for many days. The jar of flour was not spent, neither did the jug of oil become empty, according to the word of the LORD that he spoke by Elijah.
>
> *1 Kings 17:14–16 ESV*

Not only did her obedience bring supernatural provision that saved her and her son's life during the following years of famine, but it also gave her further divine favor when her son later died, and Elijah raised him from the dead. (See 1 Kings 17:17–24.)

Serving will frequently require personal sacrifice, but its rewards are profound. There will be occasions when you are called upon to give beyond what you think you possess—whether it's your time, talent, or even mental resources. These moments will stretch you, demanding nothing less than your absolute best, all in the relentless pursuit of the vision.

The phrase *giving it your all* is often spoken but seldom practiced. But before we dive deeper into the characteristics of diligence that will propel you forward, it's important to understand that without properly positioning the attitude of your heart daily, there's a significant risk of veering off course.

We must continually align ourselves with the vision. It must stay before our eyes and be the reason for everything we put our hands to, no matter how big or small the task is.

There will be many situations when someone will ask you to do something you don't feel like doing. There will be countless opportunities to be caught in personal offense, to feel misunderstood, unseen, or as though something isn't fair.

To effectively serve in our purpose, we must guard against the feelings of the flesh that can creep in, especially in busy seasons. When our bodies are tired, it can be easy for our emotions to take over, and no one wants to work with a tantrum on their team.

Be Introspective

The willingness to be introspective is one of the greatest skills for personal growth. After all, how can you expect to be a better person this time next year if you never pause to evaluate how you're doing in a certain area? Being introspective takes humility and honesty. No one likes to freely admit their faults or shortcomings, even to themselves.

However, identifying areas to improve on your own can be much less embarrassing than someone else doing it for you. Choosing not to ignore your bad attitude and quickly correct your course will help prevent the inevitable emotional blow-up you'll find yourself publicly regretting in the future.

Introspection is precisely how it sounds—an internal inspection. It's being self-aware in that you're not just evaluating your outside behavior, like a reaction you may have had. It's also taking a careful look at what's inside you, such as asking yourself, "What made me react that way?"

For example, perhaps you were short with a team member when they asked you a question. While apologizing for your tone of voice will be appreciated, your greater benefit will be identifying why you were short with them in the first place and working on fixing the cause.

Were you irritated because you were tired? How can you get more rest? Next time you feel tired, how can you be more self-aware and catch your tone in conversation before it hurts someone?

Maybe your voice was short because you felt overwhelmed by your tasks. How can you be less overwhelmed? How can you communicate better the next time someone asks you something when you feel that way?

If you've never thought of asking yourself questions like these, it may sound like some sort of dramatic self-therapy session. However, pulling a few weeds from a garden every day is much easier than waiting an entire month. It will also result in far fewer consequences.

Keep your heart with all vigilance, for
from it flow the springs of life.
Proverbs 4:23 ESV

The Bible tells us we must proactively protect our innermost thoughts and feelings. In biblical language, the heart often refers to the core of a person's emotions, will, and attitude. The careful instruction to "guard" our hearts here in Proverbs tells us that we choose what influences our hearts and, consequently, our attitudes.

There will always be many people and circumstances outside our control, but our attitude is never on that list!

If you can quickly learn to identify your negative behavior and be just as quick to correct it at the root, you will never stop growing. Someone who never stops being introspective, who is willing to admit when they're wrong, and who makes an effort to prevent it from happening again and again exemplifies incredible maturity.

Renewing Your Mind

When bank tellers train to recognize counterfeit money, they actually spend very little time studying fake examples. Instead, they spend the majority of their studying efforts handling genuine bills. They carefully examine the feel in their hands and all the intricate details.

When a counterfeit later comes their way, it's much easier to recognize because of their dedication to learning the real version. They may not know exactly why it is fake at first, but they quickly recognize if something doesn't look or feel right.

As a believer, you have the advantage in every way. When it comes to keeping a correct heart position, there is no better resource than the Word of God. Just as an experienced bank teller will quickly feel on alert when something is off with the money they're holding, you should train yourself to become aware when the wrong attitude tries to creep in.

The Bible tells us how we should act and think, and the more we understand how we *should* be, the easier it is to recognize how we *shouldn't* be. The best way to keep your heart in the correct position is to immerse yourself in God's Word daily. It is impossible to constantly meditate on the Word of God and still have a rotten attitude.

> *To put off your old self, which belongs to your former manner of life and is corrupt through deceitful desires, and to be renewed in the spirit of your minds, and to put on the new self, created after the likeness of God in true righteousness and holiness.*
>
> *Ephesians 4:22–24 ESV*

To reflect God's character, we must renew our minds with his Word. One chapter further, in Ephesians 5:26, Paul discusses the sanctification of the church and teaches how Christ's death makes the church holy, "having cleansed her by the washing of water with the word."

The Word of God acts like a cleansing agent to our minds! The Bible is the first place to go if you need attitude alignment. We are to take those feelings of the flesh and align them with what the Word says, casting down anything that doesn't fit.

> *We destroy arguments and every lofty opinion raised against the knowledge of God, and take every thought captive to obey Christ.*
> *2 Corinthians 10:5 ESV*

Any feeling that doesn't match what the Word of God says must be corrected. Imagine it as a weed you must remove before it chokes the fruit you're trying to grow. Thoughts that go against the Word will do just that if left untouched. They choke out the spiritual fruit of the believer.

Introspection can help us examine our attitudes. Pride, jealousy, offense, bitterness, and unforgiveness have no place in us and serve as obstacles to pursuing the vision.

The Red Flags of Feel

The more you read and meditate on the Word of God, the quicker you will catch feelings of the flesh before they take root. While not an exhaustive list, I want to give you the five top traps to look out for, warning you it's time to reposition yourself. These are what I like to call the red flags of feel.

1. *I feel offended.* Offense is a vision killer. It takes your eyes off the big picture and keeps them focused on yourself. One of the common ways the enemy destroys team progress is by presenting the opportunity to be personally offended.

Effective teams thrive under strong authority, starting with top leadership and extending through delegated authority to managers and department leaders across your organization.

Proper authority brings correction when necessary, whether small or big. It is part of growing together as a team. Receiving correction without letting offense take root is crucial to your success.

Proverbs 19:11 tells us, "Good sense makes one slow to anger, and it is his glory to overlook an offense." Old Testament scholar and author William McKane comments:

> The virtue which is indicated here is more than a forgiving temper; it includes also the ability to shrug off insults and the absence of a brooding hypersensitivity. . . . It contains elements of toughness and self-discipline; it is the capacity to stifle a hot, emotional rejoinder and to sleep on an insult.[1]

Having what they call "thick skin" is not one of my

notable strengths. I am a sensitive soul, through and through, so I must carefully watch this area. If another person's words or actions hurt me, I try to either brush them off and let them go or have a direct conversation with the necessary person about them. Over the years, I have learned that, more often than not, a misunderstanding was at fault.

Your leader or team member most likely wasn't trying to intentionally hurt you with their words. So if you're unable to let it go and, as we quoted McKane earlier, "sleep on an insult," then I encourage you to tap into the power of a conversation that clears the air.

Don't let it fester into something unresolved that affects your team dynamic and pursuit of the vision. Big girl pants *on*.

2. *I feel overwhelmed.* Remember, these aren't just feelings, but red flags. They will warn you of the negative repercussions if you don't deal with them. Choosing to stay overwhelmed can have detrimental effects over time.

One definition of overwhelm says to "bury or drown beneath a huge mass."[2] Overwhelm can be a very isolating feeling, and if not dealt with, it will begin to affect everything you do.

Staying overwhelmed will open the door to worry and anxiety—two things God commanded us to avoid. (See

Philippians 4:6–7 and Matthew 6:25–34.)

Overwhelm often causes you to cut corners and compromise your spirit of excellence. When your mind and body are exhausted, and you feel buried in projects to care for, it is difficult to give your best. You move from creativity and producing at a high level to sheer survival mode.

Overwhelm also removes joy as your strength. As spirit-filled believers, joy is the fuel in our tank. It is the anointing we draw from to run our race.

> *And do not be worried, for the joy of the LORD is your strength and your stronghold.*
> *Nehemiah 8:10 AMP*

Overwhelm takes a toll on your spirit, soul, and body. In times of overwhelm, I first recognize that my strength begins to feel physically, emotionally, and mentally depleted. When this happens, we must get in the presence of the Lord, for the Bible tells us that in his presence is fullness of joy. Your very strength depends on it!

> *You make known to me the path of life; in your presence there is fullness of joy; at your right hand are pleasures forevermore.*
> *Psalm 16:11 ESV*

Your new skill of introspection will benefit you greatly here. When I feel overwhelmed, the first things I ask myself are why I feel it and how I can fix it.

Taking ownership of the vision makes you an unstoppable force. You will never care as deeply about something that doesn't belong to you. That's why the best teams in the world are people who decided to not just work toward a vision but to become it.

The vision is in their DNA, and you couldn't pry it from them if you tried because it's now who they are. That level of ownership accompanies a deep level of care. Many times, when I feel overwhelmed, it's because I care so much. I want things to be excellent in every area, and overwhelm means I am wrestling with the lack it often stems from.

Overwhelm is a sign that something is out of balance. Perhaps there's a lack of time to meet a deadline, a lack of knowledge needed to learn something new and intimidating, or a lack of rest during a season of hustle and busy schedule. Refusing to stay overwhelmed will require identifying the cause and working to eradicate it.

You may also feel like things are out of control. One of the most important things you can do when feeling overwhelmed is quickly identifying what *you can* control.

For example, you may not have been in charge of choosing that project deadline that feels too tight, but you can control your time management, ability to prioritize, and what you can delegate. It won't always feel like easy answers, but the key is not letting overwhelm take over. Recognize it and refuse it.

3. *I feel unappreciated. Buckle up, baby; this one's gonna be a zinger.* It's a dangerous place to be when you let yourself think no one appreciates you. When you let the enemy lie to you, and you believe that no one sees your hard work and dedication, it is a wide-open invitation to bitterness and dishonor.

Everyone feels love and appreciation in different ways. If you've read Gary Chapman's bestselling book, *The 5 Love Languages*, you understand that some people feel loved with gifts. For others, it's spending quality time with them, or for some, it's receiving words of affirmation.[3]

In an ideal world, everyone would spend time learning your greatest love language and go out of their way to communicate their deepest appreciation to you in that exact way. It's just that—an ideal. Is it wonderful when it happens? Of course. Should you turn into a scorned toddler when it doesn't? Let's hope not.

Yes, communicating your genuine appreciation as a leader will reap boundless rewards. You will affirm your team and reignite them to go higher and do better. Cultivating a culture of appreciation will never lead your team backward.

Never underestimate the power of direct encouragement when you tell someone on your team how truly thankful you are for them and that you see the depth of their efforts. When you do this as a leader, you communicate to your team that this is the behavior you expect and reward.

Feeling unappreciated becomes dangerous when you let it begin to take root. Perhaps the initial thought is something like, "I wish my boss saw how hard I was working," but if you're not careful, it grows into something closer to, "My boss doesn't even care about me or my family. All he wants me to do is work, and he doesn't even appreciate anything I'm doing!"

The red flags of feel are warnings in and of themselves. But mix them together, and you'll be offended because you were overwhelmed, which then leads you to feel unappreciated. We must guard against the feelings of our flesh and let none of these take root.

> *Whatever you do, work heartily, as for the Lord and not for men.*
> *Colossians 3:23 ESV*

The Lord sees your diligence and hard work. Don't measure your performance by compliments. Produce the work you have with excellence and do it for the Lord.

Just as the widow in Zarephath may have felt unseen, God has a reward for your faithful obedience.

4. *I feel undervalued.* There's a delicate balance between owning and serving. When you are serving someone else's vision, taking ownership is the primary key to propelling you forward with exceptional performance.

Those who run with true excellence understand the purpose God has given them and do whatever it takes to achieve it. However, this ownership does not equate to you being in charge. Leadership doesn't have to ask your opinion about the decisions they make. (*Ouch.*)

It's incredibly rewarding to earn the respect of your team and be consulted for your knowledge and expertise. When your team seeks out your opinion, it shows your deep commitment to success and reveals the skills and valued perspective you bring to the table. However, it's crucial to understand that this is not a requirement and will not always happen.

When leadership receives divine direction, they are responsible for moving forward with quick obedience. If God gives an instruction, why should they consult you? Leadership does not need your permission to do what God has said.

It's your job to diligently find your place and complete the task at hand. It's your place to own the vision whether you were consulted or not.

This red flag feeling might be disguised as the thought, "She didn't even bother asking me about this new project," or "If this were my conference, I would never do it like this."

Building creative ideas and strategies together as a team is a major benefit of having one in the first place. If you're a leader and think your team members could never contribute to the success of a project by giving their input, then it's time to stop and evaluate who's on your team! What isn't beneficial is when your team thinks they have more authority than you.

Just as feeling unappreciated can open the door to dishonor and bitterness if not confronted, so will letting yourself feel undervalued. While feeling unappreciated stems more from your performance, feeling undervalued has more to do with your true position and authority.

When I catch myself feeling unappreciated, it has everything to do with the recognition of my hard work and diligence in accomplishing a task or completing a project, especially if I pushed through extreme overwhelm to do it.

Feeling undervalued is slightly different because it has more to do with realizing that though I've fully committed to the vision, I am not in charge of it.

Taking ownership is what accelerates you forward in obtaining the vision. It's what keeps you in the game—

not the sidelines and never, ever, the bleachers. But this decision of ownership never grants you authority beyond your position. It will never be permission to override or overrule the leadership you serve.

When you feel undervalued, the red flag warns you not to let pride take root. When you think you know better than someone else, you want to be careful not to let it fester into a destructive attitude that brings disunity to your team.

> *Pride ends in humiliation, while humility brings honor.*
> *Proverbs 29:23 NLT*

I work hard to bring value to the people I work with. I am constantly trying to learn new and better ways of doing things so that I have notable skills and problem-solving knowledge to contribute. We will discuss these areas in more detail in future chapters.

There's nothing wrong with wanting to be valuable to your team and leadership. The feeling of the flesh we must guard against is the ugly root of pride when we think others should do things our way.

The opinion you have to contribute may even be the best method for achieving the goal. But at what cost will you stand for it? Disrespect? Dishonor?

No, when we recognize the grip of pride trying to take

hold, we must reposition our hearts and attitudes, and remember our proper place. *We are here to serve.*

5. *I feel overqualified.* There will always be something that you *need* to do but don't *want* to do. Not every step of pursuing the vision is full of sparkle.

No matter what highly successful organization you look at, numerous behind-the-scenes tasks make what you see possible. Someone is cleaning the bathrooms. Someone is answering the emails. Someone is uploading the files. Someone is making the store run.

I once heard Pastor Mark Hankins say, "Excellence isn't just serving the way you want, but serving the way that is needed."[4]

You will be required to complete necessary tasks and projects that are not shiny or exciting. However, they contribute to the vision and bring you and your team one step closer.

You earn promotion, and permission to delegate tasks is a reward for diligence. Allowing yourself to complain about being "too good" or "overly qualified" for your assignment shows a significant lack of spiritual maturity.

> *Pride goes before destruction, and a haughty spirit before a fall.*
> *Proverbs 16:18 ESV*

Without continuously positioning your heart, you will forget what you are working toward. You must keep the vision in front of you at all times. If you only look at yourself and your feelings, you will lose sight of the big picture.

Never let the enemy corner you mentally, where you begin thinking dishonorably toward your leadership. That's exactly where all of these red-flag thoughts lead.

The devil is a really good liar, and it's our job as spirit-filled believers to recognize his schemes quickly and refuse to play. Get out of the mental games, and thank the Lord that he sees your diligence. Thank him for leading you to increase and greater levels of skill and opportunity.

A grateful heart will do more for you than wallowing in self-pity ever will. When your heart is right, the Holy Spirit can work through you without hindrance. And that, my friend, is truly our greatest asset.

"With the mind of Christ, we tap into God's vision for us, where all things become possible. It's this divine mindset that empowers us to reach further, accomplish more, and live without limits."

T.L. Osborn

CHAPTER 04

WITHOUT LIMIT

Elephants are one of the strongest animals on earth, known for their size and power. In the early days of entertaining events like the circus, crowds were excited to see the exotic animal up close and watched in awe as such a large creature performed in submission.

An interesting story describes how a baby elephant was shackled around its leg and tied to a stake when it was taken into captivity. At first, the baby elephant struggled, trying to break free from the chain. However, it soon learned that any attempt to escape was useless.

As the elephant grew older and stronger, it still believed it couldn't break free. Despite having the size and strength to easily break the chain or uproot the stake to which it was attached, the adult elephant never tried because it had learned as a baby that it was powerless.

Even with the strength and capability as an adult to break free with little effort, its learned captivity still kept it bound by the imaginary constraints of the past. We, too, can often find ourselves shaping our behavior based on past experiences and limiting beliefs that are not true.

Throughout Scripture, the Bible instructs us to guard our minds and control our thoughts. Why? What we think determines what we believe, and what we believe determines what we say.

Our words are one of the most powerful tools we have at our disposal. Words are weapons of mass destruction—to our enemy or our future. What we choose to destroy with them is up to us.

Words build our realities because we are created in the image of God, who spoke everything into existence. Your mind has unlimited potential.

Confess the Word

When Kenneth E. Hagin was in his eighties, he was still healthy and strong. People who knew him and heard him preach would tell you he had a remarkable memory. Even at his late age, he could recall the specific details of a story or moment in time.

He once shared how he had started to forget things in his fifties. He had read a medical journal that said millions of cells in our brains die every day. He didn't realize it then, but those words got into his spirit, and he started to forget.

TIFFANY FARLEY

So he asked the Lord, "What is happening to me?" And the Lord said, "You read that article, and you believed it." He repented and asked the Lord what he should do.

He said the Lord told him, "Confess my Word. My Word says that you have the mind of Christ, and the mind of Christ never forgets." So Brother Hagin started to confess that he had the mind of Christ, and that was how his memory remained sharp for the rest of his life.[1]

Proverbs 18:21 tells us that death and life are in the power of the tongue. How often do you limit yourself by the words you say?

True Ministry Moves

Nothing I do in ministry—whether in media or administration—is anything I went to school for. None of my business ventures came from college or university training.

While learning about the Pentateuch in Bible college attributed to a stronger theological foundation, it doesn't exactly come in handy when I need to set up a livestream on location or build a website.

One of the most important lessons my pastor has taught me is that the Holy Spirit is my teacher.

> *But the Helper, the Holy Spirit, whom*
> *the Father will send in my name, he will*

71

*teach you all things and bring to your re-
membrance all that I have said to you.*
                                    John 14:26 ESV

I do so many things today in my role that, when first introduced, felt comparable to climbing Mount Everest. One of the quickest things you will learn inside our team is that as soon as you become comfortable with one new thing, something else is on the way to shake things up.

True ministry moves. We are not stagnant nor stale in what God has called us to do, and rivers are never the same for long. They are always moving toward something bigger. We stay ready and willing for any opportunity God says is ours.

My pastor is multi-talented and has many skills. If he could clone himself, he probably wouldn't need a team. He is capable of doing all that we do.

Whether building websites, designing graphics, editing videos, playing multiple instruments, or even creating digital courses, he taught himself whatever was needed to do the job.

While growing up in his father's ministry and after attending Bible school, he had to teach himself how to do things for his multiple roles. This background of always being a student has set the standard for our team.

We are each self-motivated to learn new skills. Our

leadership has created a culture of always learning and a personal desire to increase our gifts. No team member does only one thing. We are all multi-faceted in our roles.

I am so thankful for this foundation because it removes all limitations from our potential as a team. I know how to do more things than I ever dreamed possible, and even as I write this book to you, I know it's the smallest I'll ever be. If you told me five years ago all the things I would be doing for the ministry today, I am not sure I would have believed you.

Too often, people hold themselves back from what they could be or accomplish. They make excuses for their lack of experience, time, or even age. You're never too young to do what God has purposed, nor are you ever too old.

Author and leader in the entrepreneurial space, Marie Forleo, is famous for saying, "Everything is figure-outable."[2] We live in an age where the knowledge of the world is at our fingertips. There is nothing you can't learn and nothing you can't figure out. There is only ever overcoming the laziness or refusal to do so.

The Advantage

Beyond the significant amount of natural resources available to us, we have the ultimate advantage as believers. We have the Holy Spirit as our teacher and the mind of Christ.

> *"For who has understood the mind of the Lord so as to instruct him?" But we have the mind of Christ.*
>
> 1 Corinthians 2:16 ESV

We have access to God's mind! We never have to stay limited within our natural understanding. When something feels too difficult, we can ask the Holy Spirit for help and confess that we have the mind of Christ.

Nothing is too complicated to learn. Gaining a revelation of this truth as you take ownership of the vision will catapult you to new levels. In the natural, it can be easy to look at an advancing technology or a new way of doing something in your job and feel confused or overwhelmed.

When I feel like I won't be able to learn something new, I confess out loud, *"Thank you, Lord, that you have given me the mind of Christ. Nothing is hard for you, so nothing is hard for me. Thank you for teaching me all things Holy Spirit and giving me the supernatural ability to learn this."*

I might not *feel* like I have the mind of Christ when I say it, but I say it until I know it! You can't let yourself be directed by your feelings when it comes to operating in faith. Feelings will lead you by the flesh. Speak the faith of God's Word, and tell your feelings to get in line.

Remember, whether you think you can or cannot do

something—either is true. If you think it's hard, it will be hard. If you think you can't do it, chances are you won't. But if you confess that you have the mind of Christ and can learn anything, chances are—you will.

The Secrets of God

Having the mind of Christ not only removes all limitations but also gives you access to his thoughts and ways. God has supernatural wisdom available for you. The Bible tells us that his ways are higher than ours.

> *For my thoughts are not your thoughts, neither are your ways my ways, declares the* LORD. *For as the heavens are higher than the earth, so are my ways higher than your ways and my thoughts than your thoughts.*
>
> *Isaiah 55:8–9 ESV*

Have you ever felt like someone else read your mind? Perhaps you were thinking about something, and someone said something that made you feel like they knew what you were thinking. In a similar way, God invites us to read his mind. He wants us to think like him. God has secrets for you!

> *The secret things belong to the* LORD *our*
> *God, but the things that are revealed be-*
> *long to us and to our children forever, that*
> *we may do all the words of this law.*
> *Deuteronomy 29:29 ESV*

Having the mind of Christ becomes an even more powerful thought when you truly consider God's character. God knows every answer. He has never had to figure anything out. He has never been surprised or confused by anything. He has never looked at a problem with hesitancy.

You have been given the mind that has never had a question. God invites us to operate in this divine wisdom for our benefit. What an advantage we have!

Supernatural Deposits

In 2018, a couple from Alabama drove three hours one-way to attend a Miracle Word revival service. It was camp meeting week just outside of Atlanta, Georgia, and they weren't going to miss it.

Driving home late that night following the service, the Holy Spirit spoke to this woman to sow her engagement ring. Far beyond monetary value, as you can imagine, this ring was very precious to her.

She hesitated to tell her husband, not wanting to upset him, but she knew it was the Lord. Her husband told her that if the Holy Spirit was leading her, she should be obedient.

Confident it was divine instruction, they returned to Georgia for another night, ready to sow their seed. It felt painful at first to consider giving up something that meant so much to her. However, she knew it was now a seed in her hand, and her only desire was to please the Lord.

God will never ask you to sow something of value to take something away from you and make you less. God is always trying to get something *to you*. If you can learn this, your sowing will never be the same!

After the service, she faithfully sowed it. (*Her ring was later given back to her!*) All she knew was that she had been obedient, which was all that mattered.

In the weeks following the sowing of that significant seed, the Holy Spirit began dropping stock market terms in her spirit. She described it like a coin dropping into a vending machine.

Despite having no prior experience or desire to learn about trading, she would find herself just "knowing" these technical terms that she had never heard.

Sometimes, she received these new words during prayer, while other times, a new term would drop in her spirit while she was simply in the anointing at church.

After receiving one of these new words in her spirit, she would spend hours studying each term's depths until she fully comprehended it. It was as if the Lord were saying, "Study this part next."

This process continued as the Holy Spirit taught her well-experienced stock market concepts, such as how to use charting software, read Japanese candlesticks, and read multiple technical indicators. He taught her how to comprehend futures trading, stock trading, investing, and bonds. The Holy Spirit led her word by word, one at a time.

Still, to this day, she is learning by the leading of the Holy Spirit. She describes the stock market and trading as one of the most complex and challenging things she has ever learned, yet she would know nothing of it if not for his guidance and being supernaturally led.

Her obedience brought supernatural direction that would abundantly increase her and her family. He is the God of multiplication! The Lord has given her a vision of where he is taking her, and she is diligently pursuing it.

Notice she didn't tell the Lord the stock market is too confusing for someone like her or refuse to study and learn. She also didn't treat God like a giant genie, magically giving her insider trading tips. No, she is instead being led by the Holy Spirit every single day by operating in the mind of Christ.

She pushes through natural feelings of inadequacy, frustration, and overwhelm when days feel hard, and understanding seems out of reach. That's where most people give up. Most people assume divine leading means no work is required, but that's not true.

As she told me when recounting her powerful testimony, the Lord guides, yes, but it's up to us to provide the hustle. As we learned in an earlier chapter, seeing and knowing the vision isn't enough. We have to pursue it with great diligence.

When the Holy Spirit is your teacher, he supernaturally helps you to retain the knowledge you've learned. After telling us the Holy Spirit is our teacher in John 14:26, the second part of that verse says, "he will teach you all things and bring to your remembrance."

Having the mind of Christ doesn't replace our responsibility to study and learn. I have found the more I access his mind, the better student I become. The more I understand his ways, the greater my desire to learn.

When we put on the mind of Christ, we choose to think with our spirit and not our natural mind. This is how to think supernaturally.

The Holy Spirit doesn't speak to your mind; he speaks to your spirit. When he does, we gain revelation and divine wisdom. He will reveal his Word to us and give us direction, instruction, ideas, strategies, and solutions.

There is no limit to what you can accomplish because the Holy Spirit is our greatest advantage. You have direct access to the mind of Christ, which puts you on a higher level of thinking. Now, it's time to get to work!

CHAPTER 05

SELF-MANAGEMENT

In 1984, *PC and Office Technology*, a South African trade magazine, published the source code of a brand new computer game called Blastar. This science-fiction-inspired space game required 167 lines of instructional commands to run, in which players aimed to destroy an alien space freighter carrying deadly hydrogen bombs and status beam machines.

A twelve-year-old boy programmed this game. His name was, unsurprisingly, Elon Musk.[1] He sold it to the magazine for $500.

Musk is easily known as one of this century's most influential technological minds. He is often coined America's most adventurous industrialist. He is widely known for his willingness to tackle what others deem impossible.

He recognized that he was different from an early age, though he could never pinpoint why. As a child, he struggled to pick up on social cues and took everything literally. This difficulty caused him frequent awkward confrontations with his peers at school.

As you can imagine, the bullying from this alone caused him to withdraw and find personal refuge in the world of books and learning.

His mother recalls her son at times drifting off in a trance-like state. He would go deep into his mind and be in another world, completely unaware of his current surroundings.

Musk explains that his brain works like a graphics chip in a computer. It allows him to see things in the world and replicate them in his mind. This has helped him to quickly understand concepts such as acceleration, momentum, and kinetic energy.

From a very young age, Musk felt compelled to read and rarely went anywhere without a book in his hands. His brother recalls him easily reading two books a day on the weekend and often losing him on family trips to the back corner of a bookstore.

At one point, being only in the third or fourth grade, Musk ran out of books to read at his school and the local library. It was then he started to read his way through encyclopedias.[2]

At the time of writing this book, Elon Musk is one of the richest people in the world. He has made billions by founding and investing in various forward-thinking tech companies. Most well-known are electric car company Tesla, space transportation and satellite company SpaceX, and, most recently, social media site Twitter, which he bought and rebranded as X.

Since the mid-1990s, Elon Musk has founded multiple tech companies, some of which he sold to other corporations. Have you ever sent a digital payment to a person or store using PayPal? Yes, he co-founded that company, too!

The oldest company he has retained is SpaceX, which he founded in 2002 with an investment of $100 million. Just over two decades later, SpaceX is worth 1,500 times that initial investment with a mind-blowing $150 billion value.[3]

According to the SpaceX website, their mission is to make humanity "multi-planetary" as they develop launch vehicles designed to be capable of carrying humans to Mars and other destinations in the solar system.[4]

Elon Musk is undoubtedly one of the biggest visionaries of our time. While we may not all have his photographic memory or a burning desire to read through a dusty set of encyclopedias, he is certainly an example of possibility when it comes to self-management.

Musk will tell you himself that he attributes his enormous successes to, among other things, his ability to make sacrifices and exercise discipline. These are two skills that he believes allow ordinary people the choice to be extraordinary.[5]

He has a reputation for being a workaholic, with his occasional 120-hour workweek sprints frequently mentioned in various news articles. He's known to even sleep at work to maximize his productivity when needed. He averages six hours of sleep per night and admits there are only two to three days in the year that he doesn't engage in at least some level of meaningful work.[6]

I am not looking to model my schedule after Elon Musk and his intense demands. However, given his impressive accomplishments and enormous wealth, there are lessons to learn.

When the social media platform Twitter silenced free speech and hid content it disagreed with, Musk stepped in and bought it, paying a staggering $44 billion—all because he believed in the First Amendment.[7] Diligence builds wealth, and wealth gives you influence.

> *A slack hand causes poverty, but the hand of the diligent makes rich.*
> *Proverbs 10:4 ESV*

Your personal diligence will determine the attainment of your vision. Having a purpose is a great responsibility; we should never consider it lightly. We take ownership and run toward it with the momentum exceptional self-discipline provides.

While most leadership training focuses primarily on time management, I believe you cannot manage your time effectively without first managing yourself. This chapter will focus on three main components of self-management: self-discipline, self-motivation, and self-care.

Achieving the vision God has given you will not come without the price of diligence and discipline. The question is . . . are you ready to pay it?

Self-Discipline

You will never find a person of great success who lacks discipline. It is a major key to increase and a requirement to obtain the vision before you. An undisciplined life will keep you at the bottom. Without it, your life will be chaotic and unfocused.

Self-discipline is setting order in your life and enables the structure needed for consistency. When you cultivate self-discipline, you grow in your ability to control your actions, thoughts, and behaviors in a way that aligns with your vision. It positions you for promotion!

A self-disciplined person does what they should be doing without any supervision. They choose what is profitable over what is acceptable. They are focused, responsible, and reliable. If they say they will do it, they do it. They see the vision, and they truly take ownership. Every day, they do their part to see it come to pass.

The undisciplined person chooses immediate gratification of the flesh. They are inconsistent, and, therefore, untrustworthy. Do you know someone who never seems to stay true to their word? Inconsistency builds a distrust with others. When you don't follow through with what you say you're going to do repeatedly, others may forgive you, but they will stop trusting you.

I want my team and leadership to be confident that if I say I will be there, I will. If I say I will finish a project, I will. If I say I will take care of something, consider it already done. Your word should matter not only to others but also to yourself.

What did you start but never finish? What did you abandon when all that new excitement faded? Where did others have to pick up your slack because you failed to have self-discipline?

One of the worst traits you can have is only doing things you feel like doing. Refuse that trap in your life. It will limit you from increase. It will keep the vision at far reach.

Many tasks will be required of you as you walk in your purpose that you won't feel like doing. There will be mornings you would rather sleep. There will be events you would rather not attend. There will be mundane and routine to-dos that don't light you up. *But the vision is bigger than that.*

Those who take ownership of the vision are able to look past their natural feelings. They see the bigger picture and understand how that task, no matter how small, helps to bring their team one step closer.

Self-discipline is rarely exciting. Consistency isn't very shiny. That's why few achieve great success. Not everyone who has a dream sees it come to pass. Not everyone fulfills their purpose or ends their life knowing they used everything they had.

Determine to grow in your self-discipline. Look at your actions and attitude introspectively and be honest with yourself. Where could you be more consistent? Where could you be more responsible?

Set order over your life. Wake each day with focus and intention. Refuse to let feelings determine your obedience. You are the vision, and it's time to act like it.

Self-Motivation

In the late 1800s, twelve-year-old Hans Wilsdorf found himself an orphan at a German boarding school. His parents had recently passed away, and his uncle had decided to liquidate the family business and send him and his siblings away for a proper education.

Wilsdorf found the transition to be quite terrible but decided to dedicate himself to his studies. He understood that the quality of his education would directly affect his future opportunities. He was brilliant in mathematics and desired to travel; he took his foreign language studies seriously, learning French and English.

Following school, he began his career as an apprentice at an international pearl exporting company. There, he learned many skills that would later benefit him immensely.

In 1900, Wilsdorf worked as an English correspondent for the Swiss watchmaking company Cuno Korten. His experience here taught him valuable insight into international marketing strategies and exposed him to the art of watchmaking.

The pocket watch was the style of this era, designed to be pinned to a garment or carried in a pocket. Wilsdorf was responsible for winding hundreds of pocket watches at Cuno Korten daily and verifying their accuracy.

Although some companies began experimenting with watches on the wrist, most people regarded them as women's jewelry. They were smaller in size and build and didn't have a reputation for accuracy. No one believed it was possible to make a wrist watch rugged enough for a man's use.

Wilsdorf, however, was a great visionary. He dreamed of an elegant, precise, and reliable watch worn on the wrist. Always busy working with his hands, he found pocket watches cumbersome and saw the need to create a modern timepiece fit for the twentieth century.

Years later he wrote in his memoir, "My personal opinion is that pocket watches will almost completely disappear and that wrist watches will replace them definitively! I am not mistaken in this opinion and you will see that I am right."

In 1905, at age twenty-four, he started a business with his future brother-in-law, Alfred Davis. They called the company Wilsdorf & Davis and aimed to produce high-quality timepieces at an affordable price. Not long after, he adjusted this business name to the well-respected, worldwide luxury brand we all know today, Rolex.[8]

In the early days of his company, Wilsdorf faced numerous types of opposition. Ultimately, he desired to create something that didn't exist and push past the societal norms of his day. He saw the possibilities of thinking outside the box and worked diligently until the world saw it too.

While he may have started with very little, he possessed invaluable qualities that brought him to the top: vision, self-motivation, perseverance, and an extraordinary work ethic.

His forward-thinking approach to marketing and commitment to excellence and innovation has left an indisputable mark on the watchmaking industry as we know it today.

Some of my favorite stories to read are about people in history, like Hans Wilsdorf, who had a big dream and stopped at nothing short of making it happen.

Great leaders are self-motivated. They do not sit on the sidelines doing only the bare minimum. When you take ownership of the vision, anything that brings you closer will matter to you. If a lack of excellence in any area does not deeply bother you, then perhaps you should look for another vision to attach yourself to.

A popular saying goes, "If you love what you do, then you will never work another day in your life." I could not disagree with this any more than I do.

No matter your vision, there is work to do. Just because you have discovered your purpose and are following your calling does not mean it will not require hard work. Those who work hard with great diligence will live a life on top.

> *Work brings profit, but mere talk leads to poverty!*
> *Proverbs 14:23 NLT*

Self-motivated individuals take the initiative. They not only automatically do the work they are assigned, but they also proactively seek out additional tasks without always being told what to do.

They possess an internal drive to begin tasks themselves and to efficiently go above and beyond in every way. They are hungry and always looking for more ways to produce and better ways of doing things.

When a person is self-motivated, they do not show up to work only to get a paycheck. Instead, they are motivated intrinsically, driven by personal satisfaction, a strong sense of accomplishment, and a genuine passion for their work. They strive to be high performers and achieve their goals.

Your leadership shouldn't have to watch over your shoulder to see if you get something done. After you complete a task, you should not sit idle waiting for your next instruction. You should always be proactive and the person your team trusts to catch the things that need attention.

Working with someone who never does anything beyond what someone asks them to do is extremely frustrating. Take initiative! See what work still needs to be done without waiting for someone to ask you.

When the vision becomes who you are, you stop treating it like something that only belongs to someone else. These characteristics of self-discipline and self-motivation will help propel you forward into promotion.

Self-Care

Now that we've established self-discipline and self-motivation as non-negotiable, it's important not to overlook the element of self-care. Proper self-management requires rest.

When you have taken ownership of the vision and developed your discipline and motivation to a greater level, it can be tempting to produce constantly. However, when you are a diligent worker, it will take discipline to rest.

Lester Sumrall wisely said, "Overwork won't kill you, but a lack of rest will." As I shared in the first chapter, he led one of the most productive Christian ministries. He produced at such a high level, yet ensured people knew the importance of rest.

I can recall a powerful Sunday morning service at our church. Our worship team began to sing the old gospel hymn "Nothing is Impossible," and the anointing was strong. I will never forget how I felt in that moment because it wasn't enjoyment but pure exhaustion.

It was less than a year into the launch of our church. Our serve team was growing, and when there was an opportunity to let someone trained in the media department sit in the service, I always chose one of our volunteers over myself. I felt the responsibility of being on staff and had served for many months in a row.

I looked around that morning from the side of the altar, camera in hand, with tears welling up in my eyes. I grieved the absence of church in my life. Though I was in the room each Sunday morning, my focus was serving and not receiving.

This day was an eye-opening experience that I will never forget. I was burning out and beginning to dread the purpose that once lit me up. In the following weeks, I made every effort to ensure I sat in the service.

I thought I was caring for my media team by putting myself last. But I learned the hard way that I was actually setting a poor example, showing through my actions that I didn't need to rest in the anointing—which wasn't true.

As leaders, we must always be aware of the example our actions set. It's not only what we say but what we do that matters. Serving the vision will require sacrifice, but you'll never accomplish your purpose if you burn out along the way.

A lack of rest will compromise your spirit of excellence and affect your level of care. No one can deliver their best work when exhausted, and when you're tired, mistakes are easy.

Unrest will cause an unraveling. Everything will begin to fall apart, including you. It is dangerous and destructive. It ruins your creativity and production, forcing you into sheer survival mode.

Unrest also takes a toll on your physical body and health. Life is not a sprint. You have to take care of yourself so you can do all that God has called you to do in the future.

We are spirit-filled believers tasked with caring for our physical temples while on the earth. Exhausting ourselves to sickness will not benefit your team or the vision.

Sometimes, the most productive thing you can do is rest. There is a benefit to pausing work when it's been too long, refreshing yourself, and returning to it rested and ready to move forward.

Likewise, sometimes, the greatest self-care you can give yourself is to do something productive. Many need to stop resting and start moving. Some people haven't produced anything significant in years.

Rest will refresh and reset you to the best version of yourself. An area of diligence we will cover in a chapter to come is the ability to solve problems. Those who recognize a problem and present a solution are extremely valuable to any team.

Some of the best ideas I have contributed to the ministry I work for came to me not when I was working at my desk but when I was simply out taking a walk. Your brain needs space to be creative. When you overload and overwork your mental capacity all day, every day, you limit your potential.

So, how do you balance it all? How do you run with exceptional diligence and never burn out? How do you consistently bring your best to your team without sacrificing all the other areas of your life?

The Great Lie

Gary Keller argues in his best-selling book, *The ONE Thing: The Surprisingly Simple Truth Behind Extraordinary Results*, that the common notion of work-life balance is a lie and that true balance will never exist.

He teaches that we shouldn't pursue this balance because the "magic never happens in the middle." Keller explains that instead of trying to give everything our equal time and attention, we should instead strive to be extreme where and when it matters most.[9]

For example, perhaps you have a major project on the horizon. Maybe the Lord has dropped an idea in your spirit that will require you to go all in. As Keller points out, time waits for no one.

If you try to give this project the same amount of time and attention as everything else, progress will be minimal at best. Keller teaches that you must determine your top priority and give it all the time it demands to achieve extraordinary results.

Likewise, there will be opportunities to focus on

things outside of work, such as personal vacations or a slower week with family and friends. Keller insists you will be frustrated if you try to maintain this fictional achievement of daily balance.

His perspective can be explained in the following example, "For the next two weeks, I will work additional hours in the evening to focus on completing this project. Next weekend, let's have a full family day with no work or house projects and enjoy spending time together."

When we lack focus and strive to give all of ourselves to every area at the same time, we spread ourselves too thin. We become distracted and spend more of the day running in circles than getting closer to our goals.

As someone who has tried and failed for years to achieve a daily work-life balance in a ministry that never sleeps, I believe this perspective has great value. You hustle when it's time to hustle and rest when it's time to rest. You don't feel guilty for being in the extreme one way or the other. You're able to give it your all where you are.

Don't miss the ideas God has given you to bring your family to another level because you didn't have the self-discipline to put in the work. Refuse to miss incredible opportunities because you were unwilling to provide the diligence and focus required to produce.

Work when it's time to work, but rest when it's time to rest. Take care of your purpose, but also take care of yourself and your family. All the other areas of diligence will be of no use if you do not first effectively manage yourself.

I have yet to meet a successful leader who does not desire these foundational qualities in their team. If you want to be invaluable, it's time to be the things your leader values the most.

"Focus on signal over noise. Don't waste time on stuff that doesn't actually make things better."

Elon Musk

CHAPTER 06

TIME MANAGEMENT

Increase is never automatic. This simple truth can change your life if you let it. When you have taken ownership of the vision and are determined to meet each day with the diligence required to attain it, time management is the element that will determine your daily success.

Entrepreneur and speaker Derek Sivers greatly impacted my life with the following words:

> When you experience someone else's genius work, a little part of you feels, "That's what I could have, would have, and should have done!" Someone else did it. You didn't. They fought the resistance. You gave in to distractions. They made it top priority. You said you'd get to it some day. They took the time. You meant to. When this happens, you can take it two ways: You could let that

part of you give up. "Oh well. Now I don't need to make that anymore." Or you could do something about that jealous pain. Shut off your phone, kill the distractions, make it top priority, and spend the time. It takes many hours to make what you want to make. The hours don't suddenly appear. You have to steal them from comfort.[1]

No matter how often we remind ourselves that everyone has the same number of hours within a day, it can still be easy to assume someone else has more than you. However, this isn't true. We don't gain additional time by random luck or chance. Time is always made available by sacrifice.

Those with excellent time management have sacrificed staying up late to wake up earlier. They set aside distractions throughout the day to complete tasks more efficiently.

They have often spent seasons sacrificing evenings or weekend trips to produce within their timeline. They sacrifice their desire to be lazy when they feel tired and the temptation to lose focus when the work gets hard.

I am writing this chapter on an unbelievably gorgeous day in South Florida. The sun is shining, and many people are out enjoying the afternoon at the pool or adventuring on family bike rides.

I love being outside, and I make time for it frequently. But today, writing is my priority. I am saying no to other things I could be doing right now because completing this book is very important to me.

Managing your time well does not mean you are always working or never resting, which is a common misunderstanding. As discussed in the previous chapter, it is beneficial to pause and recharge when you need it.

Time management is simply making the most of every opportunity, and as the Apostle Paul explains in his letter to the Ephesians, we should do so with wisdom and diligence.

> *Therefore see that you walk carefully [living life with honor, purpose, and courage; shunning those who tolerate and enable evil], not as the unwise, but as wise [sensible, intelligent, discerning people], making the very most of your time [on earth, recognizing and taking advantage of each opportunity and using it with wisdom and diligence], because the days are [filled with] evil.*
>
> *Ephesians 5:15–16 AMP*

Using your time well is a choice. You will not achieve

your purpose and see the levels of increase God has for you without making this choice consistently every day. Bishop Oyedepo once said, "Waste time, and time will waste you."

Nine Sentences Closer

In his book, *Someday is Today: 22 Simple, Actionable Ways to Propel Your Creative Life*, Matthew Dicks told a powerful story to illustrate the value of time that's too often wasted.

He was sitting in a McDonald's talking to a woman who had asked to pick his brain over coffee. She claimed to be an aspiring novelist, and since he had written many books himself, she wanted to ask him questions about writing her book.

She asked him about literary agents, editors, book contracts, international sales, film rights, and royalties. He listened carefully, answered each of her questions, and awaited his opportunity to ask one of his own.

When he finally got his chance, he looked across the table and asked her, "So, how's the book coming?"

"Oh," she said, looking a little startled. "I haven't really started it yet."

When he asked her why, she told him that she found the writing process somewhat complicated, that she could only write in two to three-hour increments at a time, and that she needed to be in the right creative space to do so, such as in a quiet coffee shop.

She further explained that she hoped to dedicate a year of her life to writing the book but wanted to better understand the publishing world before starting.

What Dicks really wanted to tell her at that moment was that her need for some sort of artsy coffee shop, a perfectly heated cappuccino, and smooth jazz playing in the background to author her book was a joke.

He wanted to tell her she didn't want to write a book. She wanted to "have written," and she was really more attached to the idea of what she imagined the writing life to be.

He wanted to tell her that she wasn't prepared to do the work required to produce something worthy of people's time and money, and that if she truly were a writer, she wouldn't care where she was because she would feel compelled to write any chance she got.

But he didn't say any of those things to her. Instead, he simply pointed out that she was seven minutes late to their meeting. She apologized, but he stopped her, telling her it wasn't the point he wanted to make.

"How did I spend those seven minutes?" he asked.

"I don't know," she said. "How?"

"I wrote nine good sentences." He turned his laptop

on the table toward her and pointed at the new paragraph he had just written.

"I also revised the paragraph above it," he told her, pointing to the words. "The average novel is somewhere between five thousand and ten thousand sentences. Every sentence that I write gets me closer to the end. Today, I got nine sentences closer."[2]

Too often, people wait for an ideal that doesn't exist to take action and make their purpose happen. Unfortunately, many will spend more time talking about what they are going to do than actually doing it. They undervalue the often available ten minutes and instead choose to wait for the hours that never come.

Time management could fill an entire book in and of itself. While there is much to say about its importance, I want to focus on three main components that will set you up for success in managing your time in a greater capacity. You need to prioritize, plan, and produce.

Defining Your Priorities

Many people improperly manage their time because they improperly manage their lives. Few would have a definitive answer if you asked them where their focus is. They are simply going through the mundane motions of their lives.

Not having clearly defined priorities is one of the

greatest mismanagements of time. If you don't know *what* you want to accomplish, you will certainly not know *how* or *when*.

When we are focused and know our top priorities, we can properly allocate our time and energy to them, allowing for more efficient and purposeful work.

In other words, I can do a small part of twenty tasks while feeling distracted or finish two extremely important ones.

Any Google search will yield a seemingly endless list of time management strategies available to try. There is the Pomodoro Technique, the time-blocking method, the Pareto Analysis (also known as the 80/20 rule), the Eisenhower Matrix, Parkinson's Law, the Rapid Planning Method (RPM), and the list continues on and on.

However, none of these or any others will work for you successfully without the discipline and focus each will require. Managing your time properly is quite similar to managing one's weight. There are hundreds of diet options out there to try, but at the end of the day, without discipline, a trending fad won't make a difference.

You can time-block to your heart's content, have the most organized, color-coded calendar, or even the latest productivity apps, but if you don't know where your focus and attention should be, they will not benefit you. The most powerful step you can take toward managing your time is to define your priorities.

Doing so is important not just in the big picture but also in how you approach each day. Many people waste time starting their day without knowing where their attention should already be. They arrive at work without knowing what to complete first and thus waste their morning doing a little of this and a little of that.

Working without a clear focus doesn't accomplish anything significant; it just makes you feel busy. Always remember that being busy and being productive are two very different things.

Think about what it's like when you're trying to choose what to watch on television. There have been times when I didn't know what I wanted to choose. Am I in the mood for a crime drama or a romantic movie? Should I watch something new or an old favorite?

This uncertainty can cause me to spend more time deciding what to watch than actually watching anything. The hour I set aside to watch a movie can rapidly dissolve into twenty minutes when I explore too many options. I wasted my time because I wasn't sure how to spend it.

The first step in managing your time well is to define your priorities. Ask yourself, what do I want to accomplish each day? What are the things I want to do in my waking hours? How much sleep must I get? What does my family time need to look like? What must I protect on my daily calendar at all costs?

Leaders with well-managed time have decided what their non-negotiables are for each day. Whether it's taking care of their bodies with exercise, setting aside time to read or study, being with their family, or tending to the needle-moving projects on their plate, I have found that successful leaders are not whining about their lack of time because they previously decided precisely how they would spend it.

Once you know your priorities in your personal life, it's time to look at the most important tasks of your job. What are the top tasks you need to accomplish? These will most likely include daily, weekly, monthly, or even quarterly projects.

Not everything we do in our jobs is equally important, so it matters a great deal that we prioritize. Doing so will ensure our office days are not full of "busy work," and we can complete our most important projects instead.

As a team member, I am responsible for clarifying priorities with my leadership when I am unsure. Whether this is with my administrative department head or the leader of our organization, if I do not know where my attention should be, it is up to me to find out.

I work in a very fast-paced ministry. My responsibilities are always growing with new creative ideas and projects. As a team, we plan events, launch projects, and continually work to improve our systems and impact.

There are many things I *could* be doing, but I want to know for certain what I *should* be doing. I ask for this exact clarification from my leadership on a regular basis. Asking this ensures that no matter how many new tasks I have, I still spend my days accomplishing what is most important.

Leaders should know what their team is working on and exactly how it's contributing to the vision. Consistent evaluation of goals and their progress is foundational to achieving any vision.

You need to be asking the right questions. Are we meeting our goals? Are we spending our time on things that are truly making the biggest impact? What's no longer working? What should we do more of? What should we do less of? As a team, are we making the right things happen?

Refuse to waste another day without getting at least one step closer to the vision.

Planning Your Priorities

One of the most valuable skills is properly planning your priorities within your available time. I can be laser-focused and know exactly what I need to accomplish, but if I do not plan ahead for when I can do those things, I will quickly fall behind.

When you are the vision, you carry a big responsibility to complete a large amount of tasks and projects. You need to be able to look ahead at your day, your week, and even your month and determine when you can complete your work.

Someone who manages their time well is quick to value the available ten minutes. Not doing so is one of the biggest mistakes I have observed in time management. When we know what our priorities are, the second step is to ready ourselves at any given opportunity to make progress.

I do not start my workday without a list of what to do first. I keep a constant running list of tasks I need to accomplish. There is never a question of what I should be working on or any office hours spent without significant production.

When I finish one important task, I am immediately ready to jump to the next because I have mapped my day out ahead of time. This planning not only keeps projects on track and deadlines met, but it also prevents wasted time every day. I have planned my priorities in advance. I always try to think ahead about what I can accomplish and plan efficiently.

You will never catch me boarding a flight without thinking ahead about what work I could do and ensuring I had what I needed. It doesn't mean that I never choose to relax when I travel. (*I often fall fast asleep before the wheels are up!*)

I may choose rest, but I am always prepared to produce. I have learned the power of planning ahead, and I often take advantage of a few hours of quiet focus on an airplane so I can later relax when I reach my destination, knowing work is complete.

This act of planning ahead also applies to personal priorities. As an avid reader, you will never find me without a book. I always have a digital library ready for any waiting room, long line, or lunch break. Reading is a priority of mine, so I take advantage of any available minutes.

When something is important to you, plan for those moments of opportunity. My schedule doesn't always allow hours of uninterrupted time to finish a book, but you may be surprised how many minutes you can find when you start looking for them.

One way to consider this planning routine is to ask yourself, "What can I do today that my future self will greatly benefit from? What is something I can do today that will make next week much easier? What is something I could finish right now that will cause me to thank myself later?"

Planning with your future self in mind helps put things in perspective. It's an intentional choice you make for others and yourself, and I assure you, it's worthwhile.

I once heard a humorous saying: "Waiting until the morning to get gas is one of the worst decisions you can make as an adult."

It's funny because it hits home for many of us. We have all been there at one point. We have all driven past the gas station on empty and told ourselves we can just quickly stop in the morning. But are we ever relieved that we put it off? Of course not!

To manage your time well, you must define and properly plan your priorities. When something is important to you, effort is needed to make it happen.

So, ask yourself the hard questions. Why are my priorities never accomplished? Is there something vital to the vision that should be a bigger priority in my day? How can I plan these priorities better?

These plans we make are never concrete but must remain fluid and adaptable. We will cover this in more depth in an upcoming chapter, but it's important to mention that when you work as part of a team, time rarely belongs only to you.

Coming from a background of owning my own business and making all decisions myself, this was one of the most difficult and important adjustments I needed to make to work successfully on a team with others. Every day begins with a plan, and leaders often change them.

Ministry requires that you quickly adapt and realign

in response to unexpected changes. Many times, I start my week with a plan to complete one project, but leadership makes a decision that forces me to readjust my priorities that week. Your plan must always remain fluid, or you will live in constant frustration.

As mentioned in a previous chapter, many decisions are not up to you. There's a delicate balance between owning the vision and understanding that not everything is your call. While this applies to the bigger picture, such as divine direction, it also applies to smaller instructions in daily life.

Time management is a continuous resetting and re-alignment of priorities. We each have a certain number of hours to fill, and new things will come our way all day, demanding our attention. We must constantly filter tasks by defining our priorities. Sometimes, the plan needs to change; sometimes, new things can wait.

You may be familiar with the concept of triage in the healthcare community. Triage comes from the French word *trier*, meaning "to sort, sift, or classify."[3]

When a hospital's emergency room admits patients, the triage process categorizes them based on the severity of their needs and injuries. This triage assessment ensures the correct rationing of available supplies and the order of patient treatment.

For example, a patient with a sore throat will not receive treatment before a patient with a gunshot wound. A woman who is giving birth is not going to sit in the waiting room because a boy with a rash got there first. All patients will be seen and treated, but each one has a different urgency.

Likewise, not everything "admitted" to your task list is the highest emergency. You must look at your projects with a triage strategy to know where they fall on the urgency list. Just like the order of patient treatment will adjust during the day as they admit new cases, so will the plan for our days.

You won't be able to control many things, but that doesn't mean we should forgo planning altogether. Instead, we should always plan to the best of our ability and be willing to make changes when needed.

Producing Your Priorities

Managing your time well requires you to not only define and plan your priorities but also produce them effectively. As you read this chapter, determine that you will be someone who doesn't just talk about what they want to do but will obediently step out, take action, and do it with excellence. It's time to own the vision and produce at a high level.

The Bible has a lot to say about diligence and the rewards of hard work.

> *The plans of the diligent lead surely to abundance, but everyone who is hasty comes only to poverty.*
>
> *Proverbs 21:5 ESV*

Production matters to God. You will find no Scripture in the Bible that says God supports laziness. He not only expects us to produce with what he gives us, but he expects us to multiply it.

In Matthew 25, Jesus teaches this principle to his disciples with the parable of the talents. He tells the story of a man going on a trip who called his servants together to entrust them with money while he was gone.

He gave five bags of silver to one, two bags of silver to another, and one bag of silver to the last—dividing it in proportion to their abilities. He then left on his trip.

The servant with five bags of silver invested it and earned five more. The servant with two bags of silver also went to work and earned two more. However, the servant who only had one bag of silver, dug a hole in the ground and buried the master's money for safekeeping.

When the master returned, he was very pleased with the two servants who invested and worked hard to produce more with what they had.

The master was full of praise. "Well done, my good and faithful servant. You have been faithful in handling this small amount, so now I will give you many more responsibilities. Let's celebrate together!"

Matthew 25:21 NLT

When the servant who hid the money gave it back to him, the master was very angry.

But the master replied, "You wicked and lazy servant!"

Matthew 25:26 NLT

This passage teaches us that God sees laziness and lack of production as disappointing, yes, but also wicked! God has entrusted you with time, money, and unique abilities. He expects us to be trustworthy stewards who faithfully produce and multiply what he gives us.

Ignoring the value of our time, talent, and finances by wasting their potential is rebellious. God repeatedly tells us to be diligent throughout his Word. Will you be the servant God is pleased with?

3 Tactics of the Productive

There are many well-researched strategies for being more productive. I want to highlight three primary tactics that have proven beneficial not only in my own job but also in the efforts of top leaders who are producing at a significantly high level.

1. *Eliminate Distractions.* Most of us know how to manage our time well; we just aren't doing it. Eliminating all distractions is one of the top proven strategies for getting more done in less time.

Distractions come in many forms. They can include email or social media notifications, conversations with other people, or the lack of focus in our chosen work environment.

When you work from home and are trying to finish an important project, but you see dishes in the sink, a pile of laundry that needs folding, a yard that needs landscaping, or just a shiny pool that seems to be calling your name, these can be distractions from what you're trying to accomplish.

When you're working in an office with others and being asked questions or overhearing someone else's conversation, these can be distractions. Each time your phone lights up with a social media like or comment, keeping it close by pulls your attention away from where it needs to be.

Managing your attention is a major part of using your time well. One calls it "paying attention" for a reason. There's far more truth to it than we often think. Attention always has a cost. When you pay attention to an email notification, you are removing your current attention from where it is to do so.

The human brain has different modes of operation. In his book *The Organized Mind: Thinking Straight in the Age of Information Overload*, Daniel Levitin explains that neuroscientists believe daydreaming, also called the "mind-wandering" mode, is the default state of our brain.

This mode is when our brains are not engaged in any purposeful task, and we fluidly think from topic to topic without any of those thoughts demanding a response. It is simply letting our minds wander while we relax. Spending time in this mode feels refreshing, which is why taking a break from intense, focused work can feel so restorative.

The other dominant mode of attention is the "central-executive" mode. This mode kicks in when we are facing demanding tasks. During these times of deep, focused work, the more the mind-wandering mode is suppressed, the greater the performance and production of the task at hand.

These two modes of the brain work in opposition, which means you cannot be in both modes at the same time. When the mind-wandering mode is activated, the central-executive mode is deactivated. Both are very important, but problems arise when you try to do both simultaneously.[4]

Anything that encourages your mind-wandering mode to take over when you're supposed to be in the central-executive mode should be eliminated in order to produce at a high level.

Your brain is not designed to do both, so when you move your attention away from a demanding task to scroll social media, you have just deactivated your intense focus mode, which makes productivity possible.

If you don't think your phone distracts you during your focused work, I challenge you to hide or delete your favorite social media app for just one day. Take note of how many times in one day you pick up your phone simply out of habit and try to open that app.

I was amazed when I tried this and realized how many times I subconsciously tried to open this app in a single day without even thinking about it! Seeing how many minutes I wasted in my day with mindless scrolling was eye-opening.

I am not saying social media is bad all the time. It has different roles, and like many things, as much as it can be good, it can also distract us from our purpose.

A fire can keep us warm and alive in cold climates, but it can also burn our house down and destroy everything we have.[5] Same fire. Different results.

I love the digital age and the opportunities social media affords us when used correctly. The problem is that too many people say they don't have time to do what their purpose requires but seem to spend hours upon hours mindlessly scrolling through their different apps each day.

It's time to decide what matters more to us: watching someone else's life or truly living our own.

Social media isn't the only culprit here. Let's consider other distractions that may also keep you from being productive.

Other people can distract you. You might do your best work in a room full of others. You may find yourself able to focus better knowing everyone else is also working hard around you.

But you may also be someone spinning their wheels on a big project because you are in a conversation that is distracting you all day. It may even be a work-related conversation, but talking about it when you're supposed to focus on something else will keep you from entering that central-executive mode we just learned about.

You may work better from home or in a private space

so that you can better control the times throughout your day when you engage in conversation or answer questions. Likewise, you may also find that being home is much more distracting and a more difficult place to focus. It's not going to be the same strategy for everyone.

The takeaway is to recognize what is distracting you personally and eliminate it at all costs. Anything that is causing me to be inefficient in my production is an enemy because it's keeping me from fulfilling my purpose and being the diligent worker God expects me to be.

Don't misunderstand my point. This doesn't mean that our co-workers are now enemies or that folding laundry is of Satan. *(Although I am sure I could find a large majority who agree about the latter.)* The enemy we are defining here is the act of distraction itself.

When we treat things that steal our attention—a valuable and limited resource—casually and without regard for the consequences, we will ultimately pay the price.

Small changes can produce massive results. Try working with your phone on "Do Not Disturb" for a few hours daily. Review your notification settings and decide what you don't need notifications for during work hours.

If you feel unproductive in your current work environment, instead of feeling frustrated, switch it up when you can. Try going to a coffee shop or working from home a few mornings each week to have focused work sprints whenever possible. You have the power to eliminate distractions and increase your productivity. Why take three hours to do something when it could only take one?

2. *The power of multitasking is a myth.* The second tactic for high production is understanding that multitasking often hurts, not helps.

Sometimes, doing more than one thing at a time is valuable. For example, as someone who works in the media department, I manage the upload of many different files each week. Depending on the internet connection and file size, these uploads can take hours at a time.

Therefore, it would never be efficient for me to begin a three-hour file upload and sit there the entire time watching the progress bar, doing nothing else, all because I am determined to complete only one task at a time. This, of course, would be wasteful.

The more productive option for something like this is to begin the upload, and while that is in progress, I move my focus to completing something else while I am waiting. Doing so is using my time well.

In contrast, the majority of multitasking that I am referring to is killing your productivity. Let's look at a few examples I have recognized from my workday that I have learned to combat.

Let's say you are going through your email inbox to

compose any necessary replies and take action on any needed tasks. You begin an email reply, which suddenly reminds you of a page on the website that was supposed to be updated today. Well, of course, you don't want to forget, so you leave your inbox and log in to the website.

Navigating to the page that needs the update now reminds you of a graphic due yesterday that you haven't seen yet. You leave the website platform and head to your project management software to check on that graphic request.

When you're in your project management software, you see a mention of an upcoming mail-out, which makes you think of the meeting you had two weeks ago with a co-worker. You realize you want to circle back about that new workflow you were considering.

Here you are, jumping from task to task, but nothing is getting done. You never respond to the email, the website still needs the update, the graphic is still missing, and the new workflow is undecided. You may have intended to handle multiple tasks by repeated context-switching, but you ended up finishing nothing. Sound familiar?

In a world where you can open as many browser tabs as you want, it is necessary to discipline yourself to focus on one thing at a time.

When you focus entirely on one task or activity, you enter a flow state using that central-executive brain mode.

This focus is where the deep, productive work happens. You have zoned in on what is in front of you and are fully engaged in completing that task. It takes every effort to get there and very little to pull you from it.

As Jim Kwik teaches in his book *Limitless: Upgrade Your Brain, Learn Anything Faster, and Unlock Your Exceptional Life*, "Multitasking is a grossly inefficient way to get anything done. If at all feasible, allow yourself to do whatever you're doing to the exclusion of everything else."[6]

Like our earlier example of triage in an emergency room, there's a reason why doctors treat one patient at a time. They aren't giving one patient an x-ray while at the same time operating on someone's broken limb in an effort to be more efficient. They know that giving each patient their full attention is in the best interest of everyone.

To produce at a higher level, you must protect your flow state at all costs. Stop jumping between tasks every time you encounter mental resistance. Remember that your attention is a limited resource, so guard it by focusing on one task at a time. Doing so will come with great rewards as you feel the relief of checking off each task in front of you as completed.

3. *Apply your mental energy appropriately.* We all have times of day when we work better than others. Trying to accomplish your most demanding and complicated tasks

during a time of day when your mental resources feel depleted is a huge mistake.

Recognizing when and what you need to work your very best is crucial to your productivity. It will be different for every person. You may have greater focus in the first few hours of the morning, or you may be the opposite. Perhaps you have recognized that you are the most alert and creative in the afternoon or late evening.

Part of triage is determining what happens when. I know that my focus and mental clarity reduce as the day goes on, so I plan my most demanding tasks at the start to give my best effort.

I use a different level of mental energy to reply to emails than I do to upload television programs. I also need a different level of focus to build assimilation systems for my church than I do to edit pictures.

If I save my most difficult task for the end of the day, I will regret it because it will take me much longer and feel much harder to do. Regardless of what time of day you work best, I have found that tackling your most challenging task first and foremost will skyrocket your productivity.

American writer Mark Twain once said, "Eat a live frog first thing in the morning, and nothing worse will happen to you the rest of the day." This quote is where the "Eat The Frog" productivity technique originated from.[7]

The goal is to tackle the most challenging tasks first

each day. This allows you to focus on them before other tasks drain your energy. Completing these tough tasks first gives you a powerful sense of accomplishment, making it easier and more motivating to breeze through the rest of your to-do list.

It feels great to get the hardest work done first. When we complete big, often overwhelming tasks that require critical thinking instead of procrastinating, that achievement sets the tone for the entire day. If eating a frog is waiting on your to-do list, you may as well get it over with, right?

Begin to identify when you feel the sharpest during your day and plan your productivity according to that schedule. Never leave the hardest tasks for the end of the day when you lack mental energy. Doing this will make your work more enjoyable and allow you to produce so much more in less time.

Mastering your time allows you to enjoy your life instead of feeling like you're a slave to it. Unguarded time is like unguarded money; it has no problem spending itself and will soon be gone.

The difference between you and where you want to go is how you will use your time to get there. Properly managing your time is non-negotiable in any realm of leadership and success. Determine never to let time be the master of you and steal your purpose with its demands.

When you own the vision, you understand the value of your time and its limited supply. You recognize that certain things will capture your attention while others will not. By choosing how we spend our time, we can better fill it with all God has for us.

CHAPTER 07

BE A PROBLEM SOLVER

The silence was startling. All machines in the large power plant had come to a deafening stop. Something was wrong. Employees were running around frantically, trying to get the machines up and running again, but nothing seemed to be working no matter what they tried. This problem had never happened before.

At this point, the head of operations felt desperate and decided to call outside the plant for the best local help he could find. The expert technician soon arrived and took a quick look around.

He walked toward the various beams with electrical boxes and opened one of them, seeing all the different screws and wires inside. He took hold of one of the screws, turned it, and all the machines quickly began humming again. Instantly, the entire power plant was up and running.

The head of operations was relieved that he solved the problem quickly. "Thank you! How much do we owe you?" he asked the technician.

"$10,000," the technician replied.

The head of operations stared back in disbelief, shocked by his answer. "What do you mean, $10,000? You were only here for a few minutes. All you did was turn one single screw. Anyone could have done that. I need an itemized bill, please."

The technician pulled out a small notepad, wrote for a few seconds, and handed it over.

The head of operations quickly read it and, without further argument, paid the man. The handwritten bill read: "Turning screw: $1. Knowing which screw to turn: $9,999."[1]

If you can solve problems, your opportunities will be without limit. Solving problems will open doors to generate great wealth and influence. The ability to look at the same problem as everyone else and know exactly what will fix it makes you invaluable.

I do not want to work with people who point out problems. *I want to work with people who solve them.*

Maximize Your Impact

We have entered an expert economy in which mental acuity trumps physical strength. In other words, you are now paid more for solving problems using your brain than for a job requiring taxing physical labor.

Someone who develops software solutions at Apple is in higher demand and paid far more than those mining the materials needed to build it. Someone who strategically purchases the apartment building that will give fifty families a place to live will make far more money than the construction team that did the renovations.

People who speak on conference stages, create online educational programs, or write best-selling books generate more wealth than someone landscaping in the hot sun or harvesting crops on a farm. Why? Because they solve problems on a larger scale.

When I created my first online course for other photographers, it took me a few months to learn what I needed to film the videos, how to host them, how to create a sales page, how to market my course, and so on. Of course, the knowledge I shared in each video came from years of my own experience.

In my lifetime, I've worked many different jobs outside of photography. I have spent summers waitressing and painting houses. I worked on the children's floor of a psychiatric hospital and held multiple different childcare positions, including living with a family as their full-time nanny for five years.

I've worked as a front desk receptionist at a private medical office, a barista at a local coffee shop, and even stocked coolers and made pizzas at a small-town convenience store.

When I sold that online course, I brought in more revenue than any other job I had previously worked receiving an hourly rate. I created a platform to maximize my capacity to solve problems that other photographers were facing while building their businesses. I quickly realized I was solving problems on a larger scale versus just helping one business at a time.

My pastor has often said your wealth is determined by the seeds you sow and the problems you solve.

Checkmate

When a chess game begins, after both players make their first move, there are 400 possible positions on the board. After each player makes their second move, there are 197,281.[2] As the chess game advances with moves, so the position possibilities increase.

There are more possible chess games than observable atoms in the Universe.[3] This is part of what makes a chess game so fascinating. It is rarely played the exact same way, and it is nearly impossible to map out every exact direction a game could take.

Problem-solving is like chess in many ways. It requires strategic and critical thinking, pattern recognition, decision-making, and adaptability. Solving problems requires careful thought, detailed analysis, and the ability to adjust one's solution to changing circumstances.

Learning how to play chess for the first time can feel overwhelming, with so many possibilities. Simply deciding your first move can be a struggle for a beginner.

However, you begin to learn the strategies with both time and practice. You get some moves under your belt. You start to recognize patterns and better anticipate the results of your move or your opponent's.

Like chess, problem-solving is a skill to learn. Just as every game makes you a better player, every problem you solve will better equip you for the next one.

You not only gain strategies to pull from again in the future and grow in specific knowledge about what it was you fixed, but you also gain confidence that if you could fix that problem, you can probably fix this one.

Becoming a Better Problem-Solver

Many attribute President Theodore Roosevelt to saying, "Complaining about a problem without proposing a solution is called whining." You can be a problem-solver or a whiner. The choice is up to you. Now that we've shown the value of being a problem-solver, let's discuss how to be a better one.

1. *Ask better questions.* It's difficult to create solutions based on information you don't have. When you recognize something isn't working, ask the right questions until you have the necessary knowledge to move forward.

What about this isn't working? When did the problem begin? What are the possible solutions? Have we tried this before? What is our end goal? What are we trying to accomplish? How is this problem keeping us from achieving what we want? Who has done this before?

Without knowing the full scope of the issue you're facing, you won't know the best solution to try, and you won't know the full scope until you begin asking the right questions.

2. *Slow down.* When a problem arises that needs to be fixed as soon as possible, your adrenaline can cause you to panic, move too fast, and make rash decisions. Not slowing down is an open invitation for mistakes.

Moving too quickly is something I have to watch about myself when faced with the pressure of a big problem. The weight of the consequences can feel overwhelming and cause my head to spin in multiple directions.

Take a breath. Pause. Think.

Slowing down allows me to often remember that I already know what to do next, and if I don't, it calms my mind enough to troubleshoot until I do.

There are times when I need to solve a problem efficiently, yes. If the livestream goes down, I don't recline back in my chair, and get in a more zen-like peaceful headspace before fixing it.

Because I have taken ownership of the vision to such an extent that it is now who I am, that's not just my church's livestream; that's *my* livestream. I will quickly troubleshoot until I have a solution, but I will not panic and make a costly mistake.

3. *Always have a fallback option.* When you are trying to solve a problem at hand, there may be things you cannot control in the moment to achieve your desired result. Let's take that same example of a livestream that is down.

If the internet is not working at the location we are livestreaming from, it doesn't matter how well I know the encoding software, the computer, or even how the camera feed is connected. Livestreaming requires a strong internet connection, and if I lose that, then I cannot do it.

So what can we do instead? Many people don't care enough about the vision to ask this question. Many media teams would say, "Oh well, I guess that's that."

This situation happened one Sunday at a hotel where we were holding church. Since we didn't have a permanent location, we had to use a mobile on-site setup.

Despite multiple successful internet tests before and

on the morning of that Sunday, the internet went out in the entire hotel during our service.

Losing our internet and livestream during the service is far from ideal. Our church is part of a global ministry, and people tune in from all over the world to watch our Sunday morning service.

What I didn't do was take everyone off camera and give up. We kept recording anyway as if we were live. After all, there was nothing wrong with the feed, only with the streaming.

We recorded the service in full, and after it was over, we went back to the studio, made some quick edits, and re-aired it on a quality internet connection.

It wasn't our first choice. We would have rather stayed live in the moment. But we had a fallback option. We record our services for many reasons, and on that day, we added a new reason to our arsenal.

You will be a better problem-solver if you can look at one and know what to do as a second option. *If this doesn't work, we will do this instead.*

It takes stepping back, looking at the big picture, and asking the right questions. If our first choice isn't possible, what's our next best solution?

4. *Create the margin to see solutions.* People often say they get their best ideas in the shower. All day, every day, we fill our minds with new knowledge from every direction and demand a high level of focus. The shower was probably the first time your brain could actually think.

Often, when faced with a non-urgent problem, the best thing you can do is walk away from it. I do not get my best ideas when sitting at my computer during a workday.

I can trace multiple solutions I've contributed to when I was simply out taking a walk. Suddenly, I started to gain clarity and develop creative ideas for what I previously felt stuck on—because I wasn't trying to.

Our minds need space to think through problems. Too often, we don't give our brains the margin they need to work the way God designed them.

My best ideas do not come when I am exhausted and frustrated. Remember that mind-wandering mode we explored in an earlier chapter? Calming my mind helps me to think of creative solutions.

Because I know this about myself and the benefits of being a problem-solver, I do my best to make time for that type of thinking daily. I can always tell the difference when I haven't.

Taking time to think can be challenging for people who prefer to be highly productive. Sometimes, we don't view simply "thinking about nothing" as valuable as it is.

This is why meditating on God's Word is as important

as deeply studying it. I can "productively" read an entire book of the Bible, and I should. But don't underestimate the advantage of simply letting one single verse roll around in your head until you get a fresh revelation of what it means and begin to see a connection you never saw before.

Thinking isn't doing nothing. While it can be difficult to pause your efforts of "doing" because you may initially feel idle, remember that you are giving your mind what it truly needs to function at its highest level.

5. *Anticipate needs.* One of the best ways to be a better problem-solver is to prevent as many problems from happening as possible. Proper preparation and anticipating needs are effective ways to do this.

I am a planner. My life would be in shambles if I did not plan. Planning is the building block of my time management. The ministry I am a part of most often operates at a warp-like speed, and planning is crucial in ensuring I complete tasks efficiently.

Ask yourself, what can I do today that will solve a potential problem for my future? How can I anticipate the needs of my leadership, those I work alongside, and myself? What will I need to do my job well in the future?

Learning from past mistakes will also help you anticipate needs by letting you know what you must avoid the next time. Look at future projects and events through the eyes of past ones to help catch problems before they happen.

After an event, take time to review. What was frustrating? Was anything forgotten? What is something that would have made it an even greater success? What did we like about this event, and how can we replicate it in the future?

One practical way we do this in our ministry is by sharing a running list of notes for Sunday mornings at our church. Whether it's a reminder to order batteries because we are running low, something about the schedule that week we don't ever want to repeat, or even something we found confusing for people, this list helps us identify any areas that need our attention.

We ran out of batteries once. We determined never to make the same mistake again. Create a system that helps you to better anticipate needs and be a step ahead.

We will discuss the importance of honor and effective communication in future chapters, but when it comes to solving problems by looking ahead, one must take care of the ones they serve.

Knowing your leadership's expectations and dedicating yourself to seeing what is needed ahead of time also prevents many potential problems from arising.

Know what is important to them and do everything

possible to make it happen. Always be a team one step ahead and strive to exceed their expectations.

Developing yourself as a problem-solver will propel you and your team to the next level. It will open doors of opportunity you never thought possible. Take ownership of the vision with problem-solving eyes.

Steven Bartlett, a successful entrepreneur and author, said, "You don't become a master because you're able to retain knowledge. You become a master when you're able to release it."[4]

CHAPTER 08

TAKE RESPONSIBILITY

Nausea gutted me.

"What do you mean you don't see the recording on the card?!" I messaged back furiously. I could immediately feel my just-eaten dinner rising in discomfort.

We had spent the entire afternoon that day recording in the studio. A guest had flown in to conduct a video interview with my pastor for a special production project, and we then recorded multiple television segments.

My mind began to swirl in a panic, and my breathing hitched as I tried to recall every detail carefully.

"Would you like me to use our memory card to record on?" I remembered asking our guest. "I have one right here, and I can just send the footage to you later today."

Instant regret overwhelmed me as I now considered my offer to be in charge of the content for a project that wasn't ours.

Tracing my next steps, I remembered setting up to record television immediately after the interview ended. I removed the memory card we had used and set it aside. I picked up another, checking to see if enough recording space was available.

Finding that there wasn't, I inserted the card into my computer, double-checked to make sure nothing on there was needed, and wiped the card empty.

As a disclaimer, this is usually the kind of step I try to have done in advance. I never want to keep my pastor waiting on the setup when he is there to record as quickly as possible.

When saving and backing up important files, I always try to work carefully and without rushing so foolish mistakes aren't made. However, the back-to-back schedule on that particular day required me to set up for recording more quickly than normal.

After filming for a significant amount of time, we said goodbye to our guest, confidently assuring him we would send the file that evening. We then continued to record hours of new content for our ministry's television program.

After we finished, I took the memory card I had set aside earlier and handed it to Zack, one of our video editors. He would help me trim the interview footage we had recorded and send it as promised.

It was now close to midnight, and he told me the footage was nowhere to be found.

"Please check again," I begged in the text thread between us. "It has to be there," I said, feeling more panicked by the second.

"I'm telling you," he replied, "I have looked at every file on this card you gave me. It's not here."

My thoughts began to spiral as I frantically tried to assess the problem.

I may have accidentally deleted the file before recording television programs if the recording wasn't on that card. Perhaps I wasn't careful enough and deleted what our guest had specifically traveled to our studio for.

It was all my fault. What if the interview footage no longer existed for that project, and we had to reschedule? Recording it all over again would be costly not only in money but also in time. He would have to fly back!

This mistake would affect our guest and my pastor, who already had a full schedule. If I had mistakenly deleted the footage, they would have wasted hours of their time.

The thought of messing up something so important and disappointing my leadership was so overwhelming that I started to feel sick.

Trying to console myself, I wondered if I had given Zack the wrong card. Perhaps there had been a mix-up, and the right one was sitting near the computer. It was now nearing 1:00 a.m., but that didn't stop me from running out to my car and racing to the studio to find out.

Tearing open the door when I arrived, I struggled to hold back the tears that were now welling at an explosive pace. "Please let the card be here," I said repeatedly.

The desk, however, was empty. No memory card was waiting there to save me, none to offer such a simple explanation for the mix-up.

The reality was grim. I gave Zack the right memory card but must have deleted the recording. I was going to have to admit my mistake to all involved.

I would have to tell our guest his trip was a waste. I would have to make it right, even if that meant covering all expenses personally to bring him back for a second time.

I held my head in my hands and sobbed.

Morning came quickly, as I hardly slept following the evening's events. It was time for the morning broadcast, and I looked exactly how I felt. I was still sick to my stomach over what had happened.

I began setting up the studio as the team arrived. Zack tried to look supportive as he walked in and handed me the card, knowing how upset I was.

"Even Pastor Ted looked for it when I told him it was missing," he said empathetically. "Neither of us could find it here."

I opened my laptop and inserted the card with a curious last hope. To this day, I can't even begin to describe the relief that washed over me when I saw the recording on the card exactly as I had saved it.

"It's right here," I whispered.

"What?!" Zack said as he pushed back his chair to see for himself.

I pointed to the file and opened it. It was all there—the whole time.

"No way! How is that even possible? We both looked, and it was definitely not there last night."

I will never fully know whether it was an oversight or the Holy Spirit replaced it to answer my desperate prayers. But I can tell you this: I will never forget it.

We all carry responsibility for carrying out our assigned tasks. That recording was my responsibility. When you have taken true ownership of the vision, there is no one else to blame when things go wrong.

There is no shrug of the shoulders or a dismissive *"Oh, well"* when it comes to owning your mistakes. It was not anyone else's problem to fix. I was ready to take ownership of that mistake, even though I knew how unpleasant it would be.

There Is No One Else

Jocko Willink is a retired Navy SEAL officer who has authored multiple books on effective leadership and teamwork. He is most known for his book *Extreme Ownership*, which pushes leaders to take responsibility, make clear decisions, and empower their teams.

He takes life lessons from the battlefield and applies them to everyday leadership skills. Few own the vision like a military unit on a mission that could easily cost them their lives should something go wrong. When a life is lost, who is to blame?

Willink consistently points out in his teaching that leaders must own everything in their world. If something does not go as planned, or if something is not working, then as the leader, you are to blame. There is no one else.[1]

Leaders are responsible for communicating the vision to their team and ensuring that every member understands the expectations and instructions. Leaders need to not only equip their teams properly but consistently identify any areas of weakness with the sole intent of removing them.

When addressing a mistake, pointing it out is not enough. You and your team must ask, "How can we ensure this never happens again for any of us? What will we change to prevent this error from repeating?"

When we launched our church, I had no experience leading a media serve team. We needed many new roles and positions that I knew almost nothing about. I quickly learned the weight of this role and my responsibility.

If something doesn't go as planned on a Sunday, or someone on my team makes a mistake, my leadership will ask me about it. I could point fingers and blame the volunteers on our serve team. I could get frustrated and tell my pastors how badly someone messed up. But they are not the ones who are responsible. *I am.*

Leaders must confront mistakes. There has to be an accountability for failure. Otherwise, there is no standard of expectation and no motivation to do things right. It's my job to effectively communicate how our services will go in the media department.

I can't blame anyone else for not taking a shot I didn't tell them to look for. I can't be frustrated with bad attitudes I never confront. I can't be angry with someone showing up late when I never communicate the importance of being on time.

There will be situations where something may go wrong in the media department that is out of our control, such as a piece of equipment not working properly. However, most things are within our ability to make the necessary changes to ensure a problem doesn't happen again.

As a leader, I take full responsibility when there's a question of why something went wrong. Before I look to those on my team, I ask myself, "How could I have prevented this from happening as the leader? How could

I have communicated expectations more clearly? Where did I drop the ball?"

I let those above me know how the mistake was handled and the steps I am taking to prevent it from repeating. You will not progress if you let the same mistakes happen again and again. Instead, learn from each one and add it to the list of ways you will be better next time. Every Sunday, we improve as a team because we take ownership of every situation.

If you are reading this book right now, you are a leader. You may lead one, or you may lead many. Imagine the strength of a team that takes full ownership of not only the work they have been tasked to do but also takes ownership of every mistake.

What would it look like if every department leader took full responsibility for any weakness identified on the team and dedicated themselves to finding a solution? What would it be like if no one ever passed the blame to anyone else and instead took every mistake personally? What if everyone focused more on fixing problems than choosing who to blame?

This is taking ownership. This is being the vision. "That's not my problem" has no place in a successful team. Playing the blame game can be easy when working with others. If we aren't seeing the results we want, looking for someone else to blame is more comfortable. We can too quickly look for who else is at fault if something goes wrong.

Whether you face a mistake, a missed deadline, an unmet goal, or even frustration, choose to take responsibility instead of passing it off. That's what a true leader does.

Follow Through

Someone who follows through with their responsibilities is a valuable asset to any team. Taking responsibility is far more than owning your mistakes; it also proves yourself trustworthy enough to complete your tasks.

We take ownership of the vision when we believe taking action is not someone else's responsibility. You, as an individual, are accountable for the quality and timeliness of an outcome, even when you're working with others.

As mentioned in our last chapter, becoming a problem-solver will put you at the top. Being a team member who consistently identifies and solves problems positions you for promotion. Notice you can't just point problems out. We must be leaders who follow through.

As Pastor Jesse Duplantis says in his book *The Everyday Visionary*, "Dreaming is wonderful. Doing is better."[2] Part of taking responsibility is taking action and initiative. I don't want to be someone who always says they are going to do something; I want to be the person who is doing it!

It's important that leadership can trust you to implement solutions. This trust builds from continuous follow-through on your part. You prove yourself faithful over little so they can trust you with much more.

If they ask me to do something, I want both my leadership and team to not once question whether I will take care of it.

> *His master said to him, "Well done, good and faithful servant. You have been faithful over a little; I will set you over much."*
>
> *Matthew 25:23 ESV*

Many times, I have questioned my ability to complete tasks. I had projects on my list for which I had no experience or training. I didn't know where to even begin.

I think of when I had to lay out the design of a one-year children's devotional book, or when I needed to move our ministry app from one platform to another.

I think of the time I needed to create an on-location livestream with media equipment I had never used, on one of the most important days in the history of our ministry.

Do you want to know why my leaders gave things like that to me? Not because I am perfect at what I do. They simply trusted me to figure it out and get it done. They trusted me to take responsibility.

They knew I would treat it like my own children's devotional and give it everything I had.

They knew I would take ownership of moving the app content to the new platform and only improve it. They trusted me not to lose anything in the transition.

They knew I would do whatever it took to not let them down on launch Sunday, even if it meant fully setting everything up as a practice run late at night in the studio and labeling every cord until I knew how everything connected.

Knowing my leadership trusts me only strengthens my desire to prove them right. Taking responsibility will make you a better leader and inspire those who follow you to do the same.

As the leader, you exemplify the behavior and qualities you want to see in those you lead. This kind of ownership shows how much you value the vision and will cause your team to take the initiative and shoulder the weight. *It will empower them to run.*

Make solutions and success a contagious element of your organization. Always follow through on entrusted tasks and take full responsibility for everything in your world.

"The art of communication is the language of leadership."

James Humes

CHAPTER 09

EFFECTIVE COMMUNICATION

It was 4:00 a.m. when First Lieutenant Kermit Tyler arrived at the Fort Shafter information center in Honolulu.

As a pursuit pilot, he and others needed to become familiar with the new radar systems installed around the Hawaiian Islands by working with the air information controllers. Since this was only his second shift, he expected the morning to be as uneventful as the first one earlier that week.

The air information controllers processed and tracked reports coming into the center from the Signal Aircraft Warning Service. If radar picked up any suspicious activity, the center plotted the contact on a map and sent out pursuit aircraft to meet it.

Pursuit officers like Tyler were there to learn how this new process worked since locating threats via radar and dispatching aircraft to meet them were all relatively new to the U.S. military. Their job was to assist the controller in directing the planes sent out to intercept suspected enemy aircraft.[1]

Located on the north end of Oahu was the Opana Mobile Radar Station. Privates Joseph Lockard and George Elliott were on duty that morning. At 7:00 a.m., it was protocol for all radar systems to shut down. Lockard began their end-of-shift duties while Elliott used the oscilloscope.

Suddenly, the oscilloscope began to pick up a very peculiar image. It was so odd that Lockard initially thought something might be wrong with their equipment. Lockard took over for Elliott and decided it must be an enormous flight, somewhere around fifty planes.

They both decided to report their reading to the information center, even though regular operating hours had ended. They thought, if anything, it could be a valuable test exercise.

Elliott called the information center at 7:15 a.m. and reached the switchboard operator on duty, Private Joseph McDonald. Since most of the information center personnel had already gone off duty, McDonald assumed he was alone and started to take down the message. However, looking up to note the time, he spotted Tyler.

McDonald insisted Tyler take the call. Lockard was on the other end this time, and he reported the direction and mileage, describing it as "the biggest sightings he had ever seen."[2]

The course they reported the incoming contact on was almost a direct line between San Francisco and Oahu. As Tyler listened to the report, he recalled that a flight of B-17s was due in from the West Coast.[3]

Tyler then remembered something about his drive to work that morning. The radio had played Hawaiian music without any commercials or news breaks.

Before his stint at the information center, a friend who had served with the U.S. bomber forces told Tyler that when they flew from the U.S. mainland to Hawaii, they would listen to continuous music broadcasted by a radio station on Oahu. This Hawaiian music was a navigational aid, guiding the bombers to their destination.[4]

Considering these facts, he reasoned that radar was simply picking up a flight of friendly B-17s approaching from the mainland and wasn't a threat.

During their conversation, Tyler failed to explain that the scheduled flight of U.S. bombers comprised only about a dozen aircraft, and the privates failed to volunteer that the echo they had picked up signified at least fifty planes.[5]

Having no reason to suspect an enemy attack, Tyler told Lockard and Elliott not to worry about it.

The date was Sunday, December 7th, 1941. The attack on Pearl Harbor began forty minutes later.

The carefully calculated surprise Japanese attack left

thousands dead, caused millions of dollars in damage, and catapulted the United States into World War II.[6] As President Roosevelt famously said, it was "a date that would live in infamy."

Miscommunication, or the lack thereof, is rarely intentional, but the results can be catastrophic.

In reality, many mistakes and misunderstandings on the American side contributed to the Japanese victory that day. Not one single error stands alone to blame.

As Gordon W. Prange said in his book, *At Dawn We Slept: The Untold Story of Pearl Harbor,* one cannot point a finger and say, "That was it!" any more than someone could look at a building and call one brick the entire structure.[7]

Was it too late? What if Lockard had mentioned the sighting contained more than fifty planes? What if Tyler reported the call to his operations officer? What if, instead, they did decide to worry about it and take serious action?

Perhaps it was too late to prevent the attack entirely, but planes could have been dispersed instead of the easy target they made positioned all together. They could have brought out and readied the ammunition.

Perhaps they could have woken from their sleep, known what was coming, and been ready to fight. What if the proper warning had saved additional lives?

No matter what type of work you do, you must make thousands of decisions each day. While most of these occur subconsciously, it will also be your responsibility to make decisions that have a heavier impact. Making a correct decision with information you do not have is difficult.

Partial communication is often just as consequential as none at all. It can cause others to make incorrect assumptions.

Tyler made the wrong call by taking no action. He made an assumption based on his knowledge, a call that caused him to be second-guessed and often questioned for the remainder of his military career. I am sure it haunted him for decades to come.

The Root of Frustration

When you work as a team, clear and effective communication is everything. I confidently believe that 99.9% of all frustrations experienced within a team are rooted in a lack of communication.

If you feel frustrated, you or someone else did not clearly communicate what was needed somewhere along the way.

It may have been an expectation or an instruction. It may have been a recording of what was completed or what still needed to be done. Maybe it was a much-needed acknowledgment or recognition.

"I wish I had known that in the first place. Why didn't you ask me? I didn't know that he wanted that today! No one asked me to do that. Since when do we do things that way? I didn't know!"

Does this sound familiar? A lack of communication will cause your team to have never-ending problems and will delay the vision from coming to pass. *If you want to reduce your team's frustration, overcommunicate.*

God is a God of order; his words created everything we know and experience. Communication is a powerful tool, and you will get nowhere without it. I cannot do my job effectively when communication is vague or missing.

Leaders must make their expectations, vision, planning, and instructions so clear that there is no doubt or question. When I am unsure about my leader's expectations, it is my job to clarify until I am. Without this clarity, we will all become frustrated when expectations are unmet.

As a leader, it is my job to remove all uncertainty. I must give clear instructions and never assume my team knows something I never said. Assumptions often lead to problems.

Don't assume. *Ask.*

5 Communication Mistakes

The ability to communicate effectively is a skill anyone can improve. Like many other characteristics of diligence, becoming an excellent communicator is not something you arrive at and never need to work on again.

I avoid feeling frustrated at all costs and prefer to enjoy my work and the people I do it with. Because I understand a lack of communication will do nothing but frustrate me or someone else, I am constantly evaluating how we can communicate better as a team and what I can do to help make that happen.

We all want our teams to function successfully, whether we are in leadership or not, and effective communication is a crucial building block of that success.

Avoid making the following mistakes to prevent frustration and improve the efficiency and effectiveness of your team's work.

Mistake #1: Providing unclear or vague instructions. A lack of clarity in communication leads to misunderstandings and mistakes.

When you're unclear about how you want something done, when you want it completed, or whose responsibility it is, it frustrates those left to figure it out. You'll feel the same frustration if your expectations are then not met.

When assigning someone a task, it's important to be as specific and detailed as possible.

Mistake #2: Not explaining the end goal. Be sure to always define the objective of what you want to accomplish. Clarifying the purpose of the task at hand provides a greater understanding.

Knowing the end goal of a project I am working on is beneficial. It helps me properly consider additional details and ideas for the best direction.

Clarity about the end goal will also help identify gaps or missing pieces in the project. Knowing the end goal helps me fulfill the instructions to the best of my abilities because I can keep the purpose in mind.

Mistake #3: A lack of follow-up. Following up is especially important when your team is moving quickly. It can be easy to forget or miss things when we are busy. Checking in and "closing the loop" will help you communicate better.

When I give instructions, I need to follow up to confirm that I communicated clearly. I also need to ensure any written communication is acknowledged and remain available to offer further clarification if needed.

When I receive instruction, it is likewise my responsibility to communicate any questions I have, notify of any issues or delays, and, upon completion, "close the loop" by communicating that the task or project is complete.

This clear communication prevents projects and tasks from remaining unfinished and forgotten.

Mistake #4: Only communicating one-on-one. While there is a place for individual conversations on a team, problems arise when all communication happens this way.

When you communicate as a group, there is greater clarity and accountability. It informs the entire team about the current projects, who is responsible, and what to tackle next.

Our team has a lead administrator who serves directly under our pastors. She manages all projects and oversees our staff.

If our team only communicates individually about important projects, our manager will have difficulty doing her job effectively.

She cannot check in on tasks she knows nothing about, prevent a missed deadline for something she was unaware of, or ensure we each have what we need if we never communicate as a team.

When I was a kid, my friends and I used to play a popular game called "telephone." The first person would come up with a silly phrase or tongue-twister and whisper it to the person beside them. They would continue by trying to whisper the same phrase to the person beside them, and so on. When the last person received the message, they would say it out loud.

Of course, by the time the message got to the last person, they were hardly ever the same words. It would make everyone laugh at how it had changed from person to person. The bigger the group, the bigger the difference would be.

This game is fun for children, but it can be very frustrating as an adult when important communication occurs similarly. By the time the instruction gets to the last person, it's often very different from what was initially said.

Communicate as a group as often as possible and keep important project information readily available to anyone who needs it. Doing so will increase accountability and efficiency and help prevent frustration when everyone is properly informed.

Mistake #5: Not having a system for it. We will cover how proper systems catapult you ahead in the next chapter, but this topic could not be left out when discussing the biggest mistakes often made in communication.

Communication itself is vital to your team's success. However, organized communication that you can quickly locate for reference and accountability changes the game.

William H. Whyte, author of *The Organization Man*, once said, "The great enemy of communication, we find, is the illusion of it."[8] Thinking something was communicated when it wasn't will be incredibly frustrating for you and your team.

Imagine we're setting up for a Sunday morning service, and I ask our graphic designer—who's already focused on another task—for a specific design asset I need for the upcoming week.

That is not an effective way to communicate. There is no paper trail or proof that it was said, which means there is no accountability. It also sets him up for failure if he's in the middle of another task and unable to make note of it.

Without a communication system, things will be messy. No one will know where to find the necessary information or when tasks are due. Your team will not know where to record information, who to give it to, or how. There will be never-ending questions about responsibility and expectations.

Demanding communication from your team is not enough. You must create the parameters for it by telling them where the information needs to go, how to do it, and to whom to communicate it.

As a leader, you are responsible for setting your team up for success by expecting proper communication and creating and enforcing a powerful system that cultivates it.

While missing a deadline or making the wrong decision because you didn't have the right information doesn't (usually) contribute to a world war, it will repeatedly frustrate you and your team.

Effective communication is worth the time and effort. Leading and being part of a team that executes projects efficiently in a frustration-free environment will accelerate the vision.

CHAPTER 10

THE POWER OF SYSTEMS

Can an automobile be built in less than two hours? In 1914, Henry Ford began producing cars with an unheard-of efficiency at the Highland Park assembly plant just outside of Detroit, Michigan. What was initially assembled in twelve hours now took only ninety-three minutes.

Many people mistakenly believe Henry Ford to be the inventor of the automobile. While that distinction belongs to Karl Benz of Germany, Ford was a very innovative man who revolutionized the automobile industry.[1]

In 1908, Henry Ford introduced the Model T. Nicknamed the "everyman's car," it was a simple, sturdy, and relatively inexpensive automobile, but not as affordable as he wanted it to be.[2]

The first Model T cost around $850, approximately $21,000 in today's currency.[3] Ford's goal was to make these cars available to average Americans. The price would need to come down even further for that to happen. The only way he knew to do this was to build them more efficiently.[4]

Ford felt inspired by the continuous-flow production methods observed in flour mills, canneries, and industrial bakeries. He even observed Chicago's meat-packing plants and their line-like process of disassembling animal carcasses. Ford began to implement this concept of moving lines for various stages of the manufacturing process.[5]

He broke down the Model T production into eighty-four specific steps and trained each of his workers to do just one. This specialization significantly reduced the time required to assemble a car to only ninety-three minutes.[6]

Over time, the assembly line process improved efficiency, thus increasing profits. In total, the Ford Motor Company produced fifteen million Model Ts.[7]

Ford's assembly-line methods quickly spread throughout the automotive sector and beyond, influencing various manufacturing industries.

Henry Ford examined his company and identified what wasn't working. He knew that to increase his profits, he had to produce and sell more cars while reducing the time and labor required to make them.

So, he created a better system that would allow them to work smarter and faster while consistently producing the same results.

Learning from Ford's assembly line success, the founding brothers of McDonald's implemented the "Speedee Service System," which mechanized the kitchen of their roadside burger shack.

Each member of their twelve-person team specialized in a single task, and much of the food was preassembled. It was a system that allowed McDonald's to prepare its food quickly and even ahead of time when someone placed an order.[8]

This new system was entirely different from what other restaurants were doing then. Instead of relying on a skilled cook to quickly prepare food, it utilized many unskilled workers, each performing one specific task in the food preparation process.

These efforts significantly lowered the cost of labor and food. The entire process became automated, transforming into a factory-like operation.[9] This would later allow McDonald's to expand and franchise successfully because the systems could remain the same.

Companies like Ford and McDonald's have experienced extraordinary success because they leveraged the systems they needed to expand far beyond where they were.

They refused to be nostalgic about what used to work and were unafraid to try new innovative ideas that would bring their company exponential growth.

Developing efficient systems overhauled their companies' production, which in turn skyrocketed their financial profits and opportunities for expansion.

There's Always a Better Way

If you want your team to be more efficient, you need systems. Systems allow you to do more in less time by streamlining processes and reducing redundancies.

By definition, a system is simply a series of steps that, when followed, produce a predictable and consistent outcome. A system can include something as simple as a step-by-step instructional document or multiple software automations for high-level productivity.

The goal of any system, whether simple or complex, is to clearly map out and define how to complete a task or project the same way each time, in the most efficient way possible.

Implementing systems removes confusion and frustration because they provide clearly defined procedures that consistently provide the desired outcome.

Systems are especially important when working as a team. A clear "way of doing things" is an incredibly valuable asset for productivity and impact.

When workflows are unclear and undecided, you waste time repeatedly starting from scratch. Systems create clear guidelines for managing projects and completing tasks.

When information is scattered and difficult to locate, it creates a sense of chaos and hinders task completion. Systems are essential to organize information, making it easily accessible and ensuring everyone can find what they need to accomplish their tasks efficiently.

If your team struggles to grow because no one has the time to create or implement new ideas, it is a good indicator that you need better systems. Effective systems free up time and resources, enabling your team to focus on creative and strategic projects that create opportunities for increase.

Systems ultimately create growth. They will save you time, frustration, and money. Why would you pay an employee to do the same thing over and over when there instead could be a system for it? Why stay in the same place for years because "it's the way you've always done things"?

Remember, there are better ways to do anything. Creating systems is simply examining something and asking, "How can we do this better?"

It asks, "How can we do this more efficiently? What could save us time? Have we recorded the steps so anyone could do them? Can any of these steps be automated? What would make this less frustrating? How could we achieve greater results? Who else is doing this, and what can we learn from them?"

Working without systems is like trying to chop wood with a dull axe.

> *If the axe is dull and he does not sharpen its edge, then he must exert more strength; but wisdom [to sharpen the axe] helps him succeed [with less effort].*
> Ecclesiastes 10:10 AMP

You can exhaust your efforts until you have nothing left to give and make little to no impact. *Or you can sharpen the edge.*

Maybe you're reading this, and you feel like you're drowning. Your never-finished to-do list perpetuates a constant feeling of never being or doing enough. Perhaps your project management feels far from managed; you're just trying to keep your head above water every day.

Or maybe you're reading this and struggling with your output. You feel like you're just spinning your wheels in your production. You work hard but never see the results you're looking for. You question why you aren't able to complete more projects and why everything seems to take you and your team so long.

Perhaps you're a leader who feels frustrated by your

team's lack of productivity and is looking for answers. Your office often feels chaotic, and everything important seems to be trapped in the minds of your best team members.

To advance to the next level, you must value efficiency. Wasted time is an enemy of your purpose. Disorganization steals time from leaders and teams alike.

Managing your time and implementing systems go hand in hand. Without managing your time, you will never be able to work with the systems you create, and in turn, systems play a crucial role in maximizing both your time and efforts. Both are important to the attainment of your vision.

Information Overload

We live in an age of information overload. We have unlimited opportunities, knowledge, and resources at our fingertips.

When I wanted to learn more about a topic to share with you in this book, I did not have to drive to the local library and search endless card catalogs to locate a stack of books.

I didn't have to spend the next hour at the photocopy machine copying individual pages to bring home a stack of papers to later sort through with a highlighter. (*Did*

I just make you nostalgic? Let me tell you about my college years, kids.)

Thankfully, we now live in a time when a quick online search brings up any book I could think of. With just a few clicks, I can easily (*a little too easily, according to my wallet*) purchase that book and be reading within minutes.

Forget the photocopy machine. I use a system that allows me to organize all highlighted text in any book as I read it. Highlighted annotations become categorized and searchable for future recall and reference. My love of reading has been helping me prepare to write this book for years.

So, when I wanted to tell you the story of Henry Ford and how he revolutionized the assembly line, which skyrocketed his company's efficiency, it was easy because I have a system. Or how Elon Musk read every book in his local library as a child? I knew where to quickly find that.

Because I have a system, I didn't have to start from scratch when I stepped out in obedience to begin writing. I have a system for taking notes and personal study that I have been able to pull from for every chapter you've read so far.

Systems allow you to be steps ahead. They help you organize all the information you consume and create daily and efficiently reference it.

As Tiago Forte explains in his book *Building a Sec-*

ond Brain, your success in the workplace depends on your ability to manage information correctly, and proper systems allow you to do this well.[10]

Building Systems

Whether you currently work with no systems or want to increase your efficiency by implementing additional structure, the following will help you know where to begin.

1. *Define the problem areas.* First, create a list of areas within your organization or personal workflow that could be operating more efficiently.

Ask yourself, what is taking too much time to accomplish? Where are the bottlenecks in this department? What important projects can only be handled by one team member because there's no recorded way of doing that task? What areas feel chaotic?

What tasks are often forgotten and hard to keep track of? Which areas include team projects, and are there gaps in workflow communication? What is consistently causing an issue?

One of the most powerful questions you can ask any area of your organization is, "What about this isn't working?" It's more than identifying *where* you need a system;

it's also defining *why*. This question will help you in the later steps of creating your solution.

Create a list of all the areas currently operating without a system or areas that may need a better one. Depending on the size of your organization, you can do this one department at a time.

2. *Prioritize your list.* While it may be tempting to overhaul everything you do at once, creating effective systems that serve you well in the long run takes time and patience. Prioritizing will prevent overwhelm.

Look at the list you made above and pinpoint which problem areas affect your vision the most. For example, as a church, this might involve creating a system for your first-time guests.

If you lack a system for following up with your visitors, how do you expect them to return? Are you leaving it up to hope and chance? This area directly affects the growth of your church and should be listed as a priority.

You may have an area of project management that needs a system. In our ministry, as our team grew, we needed a better system for requesting and accessing graphics from our team designer.

Before our new system, team members asked for graphics inconsistently in many different places, making it difficult for him to track who needed what and when.

This lack of organization created problems, such as our designer needing to complete graphics on time, team members being unable to locate what they needed, and people assuming someone else had already requested what they were waiting on. The entire team began to feel frustrated because we needed a better system.

We use graphics for marketing events and essential information on our website, social media, email campaigns, and more. Therefore, creating a system that served our team better so we could produce at a higher level was a priority.

Though some areas may seem small in the big picture, anything that steals time and creates irritation within your team is worth fixing.

You will attain your vision through many small, consistent steps. No one looks at a puzzle and considers one of its pieces irrelevant to its completion. All the pieces make a difference in the final result, no matter how small.

Keep the length of your list manageable and avoid creating too many systems at once. Doing so is especially important if you are a leader who needs your team to be on board with something different from what they have been used to.

Start with what affects your vision the most, and prioritize from there. Every minute saved in a system is a minute allotted for progress.

3. *Map out your solution.* A system is just that—a solution. When you think of your systems as solutions to your greatest frustrations instead of "another new thing you must learn," it keeps your mindset in a place of productivity.

Yes, there is a process to changing how you do something, and sometimes it can feel like it's taking more time at first, but remember what it will save you in the end. When creating effective systems, you must often slow down to speed up.

Consider your system as a solution map. Define your end goal and work backward from there. Ask yourself, what would this ideally look like? What steps are needed to achieve the goal and provide the results we are looking for? Does this system solve each of the problems we currently experience? Is this the most efficient workflow for our team?

Starting with the highest priority, begin to map out your system solution. This map may be as simple as a checklist template for your team or a more in-depth system that uses software and automation.

Focus on implementing one system at a time to eliminate the problems and frustrations you first identified.

4. *Clear communication and responsibilities.* Every step of your system needs to have clear accountability. Mapping the steps to your new system without assigning responsibility to a team member is a recipe for frustration.

As discussed in a previous chapter, most frustration stems from a lack of communication. Assuming someone will complete a task without clearly communicating this expectation will cause problems.

Part of what makes a system effective is accountability. There needs to be consistent steps to follow and assigned roles throughout each system step. Doing so eliminates the frustration and chaos that develops when you think someone else will complete a task while they think you are.

Developing a system for your team communication is of the utmost importance. Without a paper trail, your team will live in the "he said/she said" battle.

When there is a proper system for communicating with each other and who is accountable for what, you will reduce not only feelings of irritation but also missed deadlines and mistakes.

If I am unclear about whether something is my responsibility, I ask my team leadership. Assigned roles will ensure that your systems run smoothly.

5. *Ensure your system is built for growth.* One of the biggest mistakes you can make in any organization is creating your systems according to the level you are currently at. Instead, build your systems for where you are going, creating a framework that will support growth.

A good system works when two people are on your team and twenty are on your team. Too many teams build their systems for small operations while they believe a bigger vision will come to pass.

Build for where you want to go. What has God called you to accomplish? How will this system help you get there? Will this system restrict you and keep you small? Will this system break when you change levels?

As you grow, workflow adjustments may be needed to accommodate new levels. However, adjustments are not the same as overhauls. Adjusting is different from having to start over.

6. *Never set it and forget it.* When creating a new system for you and your team, it's important to evaluate if it's providing the solution you designed it for. Systems are not "set it and forget it." You must check in on them and ensure they are always working effectively.

As you begin using a new system, determine if any step could improve. Remember, systems are valuable to your vision. They increase your capacity to produce by saving you time and resources.

You may at first feel the tension of learning a new way

of doing something you've always done. But remember, the vision is greater. Those who own the vision are willing to learn new methods and try things they have never done before if it helps them attain it.

Be willing to invest the time needed to ensure the system is the best solution for that area. Make any necessary adjustments or changes until you see the results you desire.

Evaluation is beneficial when you first implement a new system and when scheduling routine maintenance to ensure it stays updated and relevant. As you diligently pursue the vision, do not neglect consistent evaluation.

Checking up on a system might include updating website pages with correct information. For example, an automated welcome email created six months ago may need to be updated with new relevant details.

Automation is a great benefit to any system. However, because steps happen automatically, they can too quickly become "out of sight and out of mind."

It is crucial to monitor what is supporting your growth behind the scenes. Set intentional time aside to check in on the systems you have created.

7. *Systems do not replace the supernatural.* Nothing we do in our natural strength replaces what the power of the Holy Spirit can do. Do not misunderstand the message of this chapter.

Systems alone do not determine your increase. Systems simply make you a better steward of what God is giving you.

In the same way that God does not give you a great purpose and vision for your life and expect no diligence on your part, we must take care of what he gives us. We are to operate in the mind of Christ and use wisdom to be good stewards of the vision.

Consider how Joseph prepared for the famine in the book of Genesis. God showed him the meaning of Pharaoh's dream and warned him that seven years of famine would follow seven years of plenty. Joseph suggested that Pharaoh assign overseers throughout the land to collect extra food during the years of plenty and store it for the severe famine that would later come. (See Genesis 41.)

His wisdom in immediately creating a system promoted him to the nation's ruler because solutions are valuable.

The deeply organized systems Joseph implemented throughout Egypt allowed him to create plentiful reserves. And let's not leave out the system needed to distribute such a supply effectively during the famine. *Systems are a mark of the wise.*

Remember, there's always a better way to do something. God doesn't perform at a mediocre level to accomplish his plans, and neither should we. We've got too much to do to waste time with methods that no longer work or, perhaps, never truly did.

"Don't get comfortable. You gotta be flexible. What if God wanted to do it another way?"

My pastor, Ted Shuttlesworth Jr.

CHAPTER 11

FLEXIBILITY

The triumphant sounds of victory filled the air. It was the fall of 2022, and we were hosting a revival before our ministry partner banquet the following morning. People traveled far and wide to be a part of this unforgettable weekend.

Each year, my pastor delivers a word from the Lord that becomes our ministry theme for the year to come. It is always a word to grab hold of by faith, with great expectation of what God will do in and through us.

During this service, his message revealed that God said 2023 would be a year of *transformation*. Something was about to shift in the supernatural for all of us.

One of the ways God often ministers through my pastor is through a word in his spirit that he begins to sing. Sometimes, it's a few words, and other times, a few sentences. As he sings them, the musicians quickly follow along, and the room begins to erupt in praise.

As a team, we know that if he starts humming and singing the same words repeatedly, we are about to experience a massive Holy Spirit breakthrough in that service.

That night, he began to move into a time of ministry for the people and started to sing, "Don't get comfortable. You gotta be flexible. What if God wanted to do it another way?" I can still hear the melody even now.

Let me provide a bit of backstory for this moment. At the time, our ministry was primarily evangelistic. Even though the idea of starting a church was a possibility, it wasn't until a time of prayer and fasting in January earlier that year that my pastors received the official instruction of the Lord to launch a church in West Palm Beach, Florida.

As a team, we were seeking the Lord's direction for a building, a launch date, and all the details we needed to fall into place. We had great expectations but had no idea how God would do it. All we knew was that God had called us to launch Miracle Word Church.

Toward the end of the service, our pastor called the entire ministry team to the stage so he could pray for us. These are very special moments. At the time, some of our team still worked remotely. It was a rare occasion for all of us to be in the same revival service together.

As our pastor began to pray for us and prophesy these

words of not getting comfortable and instead being flexible for the year of supernatural transformation ahead, we knew we would never be the same. Something new was coming.

Shortly after this service, our pastors knew it was crucial to step out in obedience and launch the church even though we didn't have a building. Truthfully, we never wanted to be a mobile church. We had no desire to set up and tear down every single week.

When God instructed us to launch the church, we had a specific expectation of how it would unfold. We were adamant about following that expectation, not considering any other possibilities.

However, that specific expectation wasn't from God. He never said we should wait to purchase a building before launching; he simply told us to launch.

Our expectations were rooted in our natural plans. God was teaching us to be open to *his plans* and to quickly obey his instructions, regardless of how different they seemed from our own.

When leadership decided to move forward, we began to experience one open door after another. We've witnessed supernatural growth and favor. As I write this, we are in the midst of what will be our greatest testimony yet. *I am so glad we didn't miss it.*

Many people will miss God's increase for them because they think they know how God will do something. They limit what he *could* do based on how they think he *should*.

Refuse to Be Romantic

When you take ownership of the vision, you dedicate yourself to seeing it carried out no matter what. It's no longer just a job but who you are.

Sometimes, you have to make a change. If you refuse, you've already lost.

Gary Vaynerchuk, a well-known marketing expert, frequently emphasizes the importance of not being attached to what used to work.

I've seen this firsthand in churches across the nation. Too often, people cling to traditional methods, disregarding new and better approaches. This romantic mindset is a mistake that will keep you small.

Let's be clear. I am not referring to foundational truths and being flexible about what the Word of God says. I am specifically speaking to the unwillingness to change a method that is no longer working because you're too attached to how things used to be.

You should never value tradition more than the vision. Your attachment to how something has always been should never keep you from trying a more effective approach. Our methods should always serve the vision, not the other way around.

Change is a constant for those who grow. Nothing that is alive can stay the same. If you want to move forward, you must welcome change. Change is necessary for increase, and you must see it as an opportunity instead of a threat.

"We've never done anything like that on social media. This process is how we have always managed ministry partnership. This method is how we always plan our events. We've never done anything like that on a website before. We don't know how to use an app like that. We have always done it this way."

Just because something used to work doesn't mean it will always work. Complacency is dangerous and often leads to stagnation. The willingness to try something you've never done in an effort to achieve greater results is incredibly valuable.

As Warren Buffet once said,

> Should you find yourself in a chronically leaking boat, energy devoted to changing vessels is likely to be more productive than energy devoted to patching leaks.[1]

Being willing to change how you do something can

catapult you to the next level. Even if changes are daunting initially, they can create opportunities you never knew existed. Refuse to let personal comfort and routine hold you back.

In Genesis 12, God commands Abram (later called Abraham) to leave his country, his people, and his father's household to go to a land God would show him.

Doing so meant leaving behind all that was familiar and comfortable to him. Abram would have to leave behind his home, community, and the lifestyle he knew.

Leaving also meant stepping into the unknown, as God did not immediately specify where Abram was going or where he would end up.

Despite this, Abram obeyed. He said goodbye to routines, customs, traditions, and everything familiar to pursue what God had promised him.

God massively blessed Abram for his obedience. Everything God gave him throughout his life was greater than anything he left behind. He is still known today as the father of faith! Consider everything Abram would have missed if he chose to stay in the familiar.

Attaining the vision will require setting aside your own ideas and preferences to fulfill God's purpose in whatever way he asks. It is crucial for the larger divine instructions and even your daily life as you pursue the vision.

Will Obedience Win?

You can clearly understand the purpose God has set for your life. You can be a confident problem-solver with excellent communication and time-management skills, exhibiting all the areas of diligence highlighted in this book thus far. However, if you are unwilling to change when God calls for it, you will miss what he has for you.

While systems are essential for growth, it's crucial not to let your self-imposed structure hinder your progress when change is needed. Systems are important for increase, but you must also remain flexible.

James Clear, author of the bestselling book *Atomic Habits*, says it well: "Flexibility alone is not a great strategy, but the lack of it can ruin one."[2]

Staying flexible opens the door to continuous improvement. It also allows you to regularly evaluate what is and isn't working so you don't get stuck.

When God tells you to change something, you should not respond with, "But God, that goes against the organized system I worked so hard to create." When God instructs you to do something different, you should not say, "I'm sorry, God, that doesn't fit into my schedule."

If the vision truly matters to you, regardless of the system, schedule, or personal plan in place, when God says move, you move. God will never give an instruction that sets you back or leads you into destruction. You will never regret obedience.

As a ministry team, we believe that leadership instructions come from God. When my pastors ask me to do something, I see it as God telling me to do it, whether small or big.

Sometimes, my flesh may not agree with the changes my leadership wants to make. When you invest yourself into building something and then leadership wants to go in a different direction, it's easy to feel frustrated that you wasted your time.

When a new change requires more of me, and I already feel stretched thin, it can feel overwhelming in the natural. The red flags of feel I taught in an earlier chapter are not just ideas. They are natural feelings that raise their head on a regular basis and must be put in their place by my spirit.

Always remember your proper place of authority. It's easy to have a fleshly attitude when things change, especially at the last minute. When things don't go as you originally planned, it can be a test to see if your spirit man is built up and in charge. What will win? Your feelings or your obedience?

Your flesh may not agree with an instruction, but it doesn't matter. Those who have become the vision understand God has appointed their leadership. No matter what their direction for change will affect, you never want to stay so rigid in your ways that you miss something greater.

Be Hungry for the Better

When I started my photography business, I had no idea what I was doing. I had no business experience, so I spent every free moment trying to learn anything I could online. I was hungry to learn how to build something great.

While self-learning helped, it wasn't until I started to connect myself to more established business owners that I saw a major shift in growth. I paid attention to what they were doing and how they did it. I invested in mentorships and educational workshops that catapulted me ahead.

I specifically remember the difference that one mentor session made for me. A very successful photographer in my city offered coaching sessions. The cost of booking one was a big investment for me at the time, but I decided to take the risk. I was determined to learn as much as I could from her during that opportunity.

After thoroughly reviewing my business, she told me that my business name should change. She pointed out the value of doing so, even though it meant I would have to change almost everything. This included my website, business cards, logo, and more.

She told me I needed to re-brand my entire business because what I was showing her didn't match my vision. To be honest, I was expecting great advice from her, but I was not expecting that.

I was hesitant at first. After all, I had poured myself into building what I already had, and my new business still felt like "my baby." *Change everything? All that time and money? Wasted?*

But I highly respected this established photographer. That's why I paid for her time, so she could give me honest insight on what I needed to change to grow. I wanted to be better.

I followed her advice. After that session, I changed everything about my brand. I changed my business name and hired a professional designer to make a completely new website. It felt like starting from scratch, but everything started to fall into place as I made these changes. *She was right.*

This big change propelled my business forward in a way I never expected, and soon after, photographers asked *me* to mentor *them*.

Asking how to be better requires humility and honesty. You have to be honest about what isn't working with yourself and others. You have to be willing to accept the advice of those who are where you want to be and are doing what you want to do.

Whenever we visit other churches or are around other ministries, I look for opportunities to ask their leadership and administration questions about what is working well for them.

This is because I want to ensure that we always use the most effective methods for anything we do. If someone else has found a new way of doing something that works better than what I am doing, I want to learn from them.

Many people avoid asking questions like these and, as a result, stay stuck. They remain stagnant in their old methods because pride keeps them from asking, or they refuse to be hungry for a better way.

I always remind myself that no matter how skilled I feel in an area, someone who knows how to do it better is always out there. If someone has a more effective method, I will be willing to change what I need to in order to achieve greater results.

"You cannot receive revelation and anointing from a person you criticize."

Pastor Mark Hankins

CHAPTER 12

LOYALTY & HONOR

Most people would never dream of stepping onto an active battlefield unarmed. Who would willingly run into enemy fire without so much as a weapon for protection? Yet, this is the story of an unlikely hero.

When the United States entered World War II, Desmond Doss worked as a joiner in a Virginia shipyard. Born in 1919 to a devout Seventh-day Adventist family, Doss was a committed pacifist. His faith held firm to the belief that all life was sacred, and he did not believe in killing—whether in defense or attack, even against an enemy.

Doss worked in a critical area of the shipyard that was essential to the war effort, which exempted him from mandatory enlistment.[1] It would have been easy, even expected, for Doss to seek a deferment, especially given his refusal to bear arms.[2]

However, Doss felt a profound calling to serve his

country and to aid his fellow man. When drafted in the spring of 1942, he didn't invoke his status as a conscientious objector to avoid service. Instead, he believed the war was just and wanted to contribute—but on his terms, by saving lives rather than taking them.

Despite his refusal to carry a weapon, Doss enlisted and completed basic training without ever touching a gun. He also adhered strictly to his religious principles, such as observing his Sabbath during boot camp. This commitment meant he could not work or perform any duties on Saturdays.

As one might expect, Doss faced severe ridicule and harassment during his training. Other men in his unit tried to get him to transfer. Even commanding officers attempted to remove such a "coward" on grounds of mental illness.[3]

They bullied him relentlessly. They warned him with threats such as, "Doss, when we get into combat, I'll make sure you don't come back alive." They even threw their boots at him as he spent time in prayer.[4] Even then, he did not back down. He held strong to his convictions and was an exemplary soldier.

In 1944, Doss shipped out, bound for the Pacific as a member of the medical detachment of the 307th Infantry Regiment, 77th Infantry Division.[5]

As a medic at each battle, Doss treated wounded soldiers even under heavy enemy fire. Having spent his previous training constantly derided for his perceived cowardice, he was now beginning to earn a new reputation for his bravery.

In late April 1945, twenty-six-year-old Doss and his battalion deployed to assist in a critical battle in Okinawa, located at the southwestern tip of Japan.

Their mission involved scaling a perilous 400-foot-high cliff known as Hacksaw Ridge, using cargo nets to reach a plateau. Awaiting them at the top were thousands of heavily armed Japanese soldiers entrenched in hidden caves and bunkers.[6]

The attempt to break the enemy's hold was bloody and brutal. For several days, Doss continually risked his own life to aid his fallen comrades. Unafraid to rush into mortal danger, he worked to save the very men who had once threatened his own life.[7]

About a week into the battle, they appeared on the verge of victory, ready to take the ridge from the enemy. With Doss being the only medic available, he advanced alongside the rest of the men, still unarmed.

However, as they pressed forward, the Japanese unleashed a concentration of artillery and heavy fire, pushing back their efforts.[8]

This assault left many dead and injured soldiers in its wake. Soon the fighting became so intense that commanders ordered all men to retreat. Doss refused to leave wounded men behind.[9]

For hours, Doss tended to the wounded, tirelessly dragging each one to the cliff's edge and lowering them to safety using a rope sling. After every successful rescue, he prayed, "Dear God, let me save just one more."[10]

By nightfall, he had bravely saved seventy-five soldiers, including many who had once scorned him for his "absence" of courage. Even after grenade fragments and a sniper's bullet injured his arm, he continued to treat others before himself.

On October 12th, 1945, President Truman presented Doss with the Medal of Honor.[11] Those who had once shamed him now boasted his unmatched bravery. Doss did not show honor to others just one time or only when it was convenient.

He lived a lifestyle of honor, no matter the cost.

More Than Respect

When we are young, our parents teach us how to be respectful, to use our manners, and to always be polite. Many people think honor is simply showing respect, but it's more than that.

In his book *Honor: Above and Beyond*, Pastor Mark Hankins teaches that you can respect someone with words, but true honor requires substance.[12] There's a cost to honor, and it's far more than what you say.

Throughout Scripture, the word "honor" speaks of both weight and value. Exodus 20:12 commands children to honor their father and mother.

The Hebrew verb used for honor here is *kâbêd*. It means to "give weight." Translators say you can paraphrase this verse to mean we are to give our parents the weight of authority they deserve.[13]

Kâbêd is used in the Old Testament when the word honor is specifically needed and when referencing something heavy or of great importance.

We see it used in Exodus when Moses lifted his arms in the battle against the Amalekites, and his hands became too *heavy* to hold up by himself. (See Exodus 17:12.)

It emphasizes weightiness, as in Genesis 13:2, when the Bible describes how Abram was very *wealthy*.

Looking at the original text helps us differentiate the meaning of true biblical honor and respect. Honor is a deeper acknowledgment of the significance of someone's position or value.

It is more than an outward action or feeling of polite admiration. It's about "giving weight" to someone's authority and role, often tied to reverence and loyalty.

In the New Testament, the Greek word for honor is most commonly *timaō*. This word is used in several places, including when Jesus rebukes the Pharisees about the commandment to *honor* their father and mother (Matthew 15:4) and again when Jesus replies to the Judeans that he *honors* his father in Heaven. (See John 8:49.)

However, this Greek word *timaō* is also used in Matthew 27:9. Judas had just betrayed Jesus for thirty pieces of silver.

> *Then was fulfilled what had been spoken by the prophet Jeremiah, saying, "And they took the thirty pieces of silver, the price of him on whom a price had been set by some of the sons of Israel.*
>
> *Matthew 27:9 ESV*

The Greek word for "price" used here in this verse is the same word used for honoring your mother and father a few chapters earlier. *Timaō* means to prize or fix a valuation upon.[14]

Honor is greater than showing respect. It speaks to how something or someone is valued and esteemed. It is the recognition and weight of someone's true worth.

Honoring Leadership

My pastors show honor to others like no two people I

have ever met. Whether it's their own family, other pastors or leaders, our team, or even people who attend our church—I have never known them to show dishonor. Not to anyone.

Like everything else, their example has set the standard for our ministry and how we operate. Our team has a zero-tolerance policy for dishonor, especially for leadership.

My pastors are not my friends, nor are they my employers. Do we have a friendship? Absolutely. They are like family to me. Do they employ me? Yes, and it is the best job I have ever had. But my pastors are far more than that to me, and that's where many people miss it.

My pastors are my spiritual authority. I am submitted to their leadership on a spiritual level, not just an earthly level. Their authority has a significant weight in my life.

Honoring my pastors means I do not show them respect when they are in the room and then complain about them when they leave. I do not hold them in high regard only on Sundays or when others are around.

As a team, we do not speak negatively about our leadership. We do not sow words of dishonor—not when we are tired, not when we are frustrated, not when we think we are right and they are wrong.

There is a highly esteemed value to their position and, therefore, to ours. We do not ever treat this relationship flippantly. I honor them with the substance of my life. I honor them with my time, my energy, and my resources.

The Bible commands us to work willingly at whatever we do, as though we are working for the Lord rather than for people (Colossians 3:23). Everything my pastors ask me to do, I treat as though God is telling me to do it.

It is also important to honor other pastors and leaders beyond your own. Just because they pastor another church does not make them less deserving of honor and respect.

As a Bible college graduate, I know many pastors and evangelists who were also students in my classes. I knew them when we were young, simply trying to survive the grueling college schedule and working to afford bottomless cappuccinos and pizza.

They are now pastors and leaders of their own ministries. I do not speak to them as casually as I would have years ago in the college cafeteria. They are now in a position deserving of my respect and honor.

When we travel and visit other churches for revival meetings, I am privileged to meet pastors and ministry leaders from around the nation. No matter how long I have known them or how casual the setting is, I strive to treat them with great honor.

I would never address them by first name without addressing them as "Pastor." I am not an entitled guest who speaks to leaders however I want. I represent our ministry in every leadership interaction, a great privilege I do not take for granted.

Honoring One Another

God doesn't call us to honor only our spiritual leaders; he also commands us to show honor to one another.

While I may not show my teammates the same level of honor I give my pastors, that doesn't mean we disregard honor altogether. Honor is a core value in our team and an essential part of our ministry's DNA.

> *We ask you, brothers, to respect those who labor among you and are over you in the Lord and admonish you, and to esteem them very highly in love because of their work. Be at peace among yourselves.*
> *1 Thessalonians 5:12–13 ESV*

When there's an atmosphere of honor, there is peace. You cannot stay in offense toward someone you choose to honor. When you honor someone, you are not hoping to see them fail. You cannot tear someone down while honoring them at the same time.

You may be reading this and quickly thinking you

would never be dishonorable. But as my pastor teaches, delayed obedience is still disobedience. Likewise, *a lack of honor is still dishonor.*

Dishonor can quickly destroy the vision. It is rooted in rebellion and pride—two dangerous elements the enemy uses to bring division. These two very things caused his removal from Heaven and separated him from God for all eternity.

Honor each other in both your words and your actions. Ask yourself, how can I show honor to someone on my team today? How can I honor another family in my church? When honor becomes the culture, the blessings of God will flow unhindered.

The Rewards of Honor

Honor is valuable to God and directly connected to increase and blessing throughout the Bible.

> *But I will honor those who honor me, and I will despise those who think lightly of me.*
>
> *1 Samuel 2:30 NLT*

This verse is a strong warning. God will despise those who esteem him lightly or, in other words, those who dishonor him.

Honor positions you for increase. (See Proverbs 3:9–10.) When we honor God with our resources, he will reward us in abundance because sowing and reaping are how the kingdom of God functions.

If you want honor, you must first sow it. Properly honoring your spiritual leadership honors God, and God honors those who honor him!

Honoring spiritual leadership allows you to receive from their anointing. How will you receive spiritual impartation if you constantly criticize and speak negatively about your pastor? The anointing will not flow in an atmosphere of dishonor.

When Jesus went to Nazareth to minister to the people there, instead of finding faith, they opposed him with dishonor. They didn't "give weight" to his anointing and the power he carried. They chose to be offended, asking why he thought he was better than them. Wasn't he just a carpenter? Who does he think he is?

> *And Jesus said to them, "A prophet is not without honor, except in his hometown and among his relatives and in his own household." And he could do no mighty work there, except that he laid his hands on a few sick people and healed them. And*

he marveled because of their unbelief.
Mark 6:4–6 ESV

Their lack of honor toward Jesus kept him from performing miracles for them. What would have happened in Nazareth that day had they received him differently? Whose life could have been forever changed by Jesus meeting their need supernaturally?

When you lack honor in your life, you cut off blessings and increase. As you diligently pursue the vision God has given you, determine to be an individual of honor.

Honor your leadership and those around you. Honor the Lord by honoring his Word. Give significant weight to the spiritual authority God has placed over you.

In a world of entitlement and fleeting loyalty, choose to be the defining example. By valuing honor, you will teach its importance to those around you because it will never go without reward.

CHAPTER 13

SEEING THROUGH THE EYES OF FAITH

A twelve-year-old boy wandered to the familiar waterfront along the Elbe River in Glückstadt, Germany, where he loved to watch the ships sail by. This spot was his refuge, far from his tedious chores and teasing siblings. He could escape, dream, and get lost in his imagination.

On this particular day, something unusual caught his attention. An enormous ship had docked on the pier, its towering frame blocking his view of the river. Being such a small port, this was an uncommon sight.

As curious children do, he couldn't help but approach the great ship tied so close to the dock. Large, thick ropes stretched down from the bow and stern, securing the massive ship, weighing thousands of tons, so close to the pier that he could easily touch it. It was too exciting to resist.

He reached out to feel the surprising warmth beneath his fingers. Despite the cool air, the ship had warmed in the sun. Curiosity grew as he placed both his hands on the side of the ship and pushed against it with all his might. He was astonished as the boat moved a few inches from the pier. His eyes widened with delight, and it filled him with wonder.

He knew that if this same ship were on land, he and even a thousand others could not have the strength to move such a "mountain of steel." However, here on the water, it was within the realm of the possible.

God spoke to this young boy's heart that day. He told him that when he asked him to do the impossible, he should always quickly obey and not question how it would be done, because his ways have no limit.

This young boy was Reinhard Bonnke, the great evangelist.[1] He led millions to Christ throughout his life and ministry.

When God gives you a vision, many things will look impossible in the natural. God is not finite or human; his ways are much higher than ours.

> *For my thoughts are not your thoughts, neither are your ways my ways, declares the LORD. For as the heavens are higher than the earth, so are my ways higher than your ways and my thoughts than your thoughts.*
> *Isaiah 55:8–9 ESV*

Faith makes the impossible possible. It places the unreachable in your grasp, and just as water carries a ship, your faith will set things in the realm of possibility.

See with Your Spirit

When God gives you a vision, deep ownership of that purpose propels you to exceptional performance and promotion.

The characteristics of diligence—such as managing your time properly, being a problem solver, building systems, and communicating well—are each vital to your success. But if you desire to please God, you're going to need faith.

> *And without faith it is impossible to please him.*
>
> *Hebrews 11:6 ESV*

Faith is the currency of the kingdom. In his book *The Unlimited Power of Faith*, Bishop David Oyedepo teaches that faith is the act of Christianity. It's more than a doctrine. It's a spiritual asset essential for every Christian who desires to fulfill their destiny and purpose.[2]

As believers, we have spiritual weapons at our disposal. Trying to move forward using only natural resources and methods is a great mistake. We are not like the world, and our ministry should not function like it. We are Spirit-led!

Your natural mind may resist when God reveals his plans for you. You will fight the urge to rationalize your objections and make excuses. You may compare the vision to your bank account or the size of your team.

Remember, faith is not in your mind; it's in your spirit. When we put on the mind of Christ, we start thinking with our spirit. It's a higher way of thinking. It's accessing God's thoughts and *how he thinks* so we can be more like him.

I once heard Pastor Nancy Dufresne, author of *Following the Holy Spirit*, explain it like packing a suitcase for a trip. She said, "I never go to my refrigerator to look for my shoes. Why? Because that's not where I keep my shoes."

It sounds ridiculous, doesn't it? We would never go to our freezer to find our sunglasses or our closet to find a glass of milk. In the same way, we are not to look to our mind for the things of the Spirit because that's not where our faith is.

When we follow the Holy Spirit, we won't know everything beforehand. You won't always know every step of a plan God gives you. He will tell you what you need to know when you need to know it. If your flesh is anything like mine, this is a discipline.

We naturally crave clarity; our flesh wants to see the exact way forward. Our flesh wants to be in control and have the final say, yet faith requires us to trust in what we cannot see.

Attaining the vision God gives you will require you to not only *think* and *hear* with your spirit, but to also *see* with your spirit. Faith is seeing what God has already said, even if it remains unseen in the natural realm.

> *Now faith is the assurance (title deed, confirmation) of things hoped for (divinely guaranteed), and the evidence of things not seen [the conviction of their reality— faith comprehends as fact what cannot be experienced by the physical senses].*
>
> *Hebrews 11:1 AMP*

Just as putting on the mind of Christ allows us to think like God thinks, seeing with eyes of faith will enable us to see what he sees.

In 1 Kings 18, the prophet Elijah defeated the prophets of Baal in a great showdown, proving that the God of Israel was the only true living God. The nation had been in a severe drought for three years, and God told Elijah that he was going to send rain.

After the fire consumed the sacrifice on the altar, God proved himself once again. Elijah told King Ahab, "Go up, eat and drink, for there is a sound of the rushing of rain" (1 Kings 18:41). Elijah could already hear what was coming in his spirit. *Now, it was time to see it.*

> *So Ahab went up to eat and to drink. And Elijah went up to the top of Mount Carmel. And he bowed himself down on the earth and put his face between his knees. And he said to his servant, "Go up now, look toward the sea." And he went up and looked and said, "There is nothing." And he said, "Go again," seven times.*
>
> *1 Kings 18:42–43 ESV*

Elijah had the faith to see what he heard. A few verses earlier, we read that God told him he would send rain to the earth. (See 1 Kings 18:1.) He sent his servant to look for the cloud in the sky. He was expecting him to see the evidence of what they were believing for by faith—what he already knew to be true.

His servant went out and looked as instructed but returned to tell him that he saw nothing. Elijah would not accept this as truth. He sent him back to look seven times. If God had said it, he would see it.

> *The seventh time the servant said, "Look, a small cloud, the size of the palm of a man's hand, is rising up from the sea." Elijah then said, "Go and tell Ahab, 'Hitch up the chariots and go down, so that the rain won't overtake you.'"*
>
> *1 Kings 18:44 NET*

When God gives you a vision, you have to see it through the eyes of faith. You must know that what God has revealed to you in your spirit will come to pass even if you can't see it in the natural realm yet.

Having a vision means knowing where you are going and what God has called you to do. You hear it in your spirit, and you see it through the eyes of faith.

If you can see what is happening in the supernatural realm, the cares of this natural world become of little consequence. What you see in your spirit becomes the higher reality.

In 2 Kings 6, the king of Syria was at war with Israel. Despite several attempts to invade and overtake them, God warned the prophet Elisha in his spirit ahead of time, and he told the king of Israel to be on guard.

Frustrated by his failed tactics, the king of Syria summoned his advisors to find out why his plans kept failing. When one of them revealed that the prophet Elisha was the cause, the king sent orders to capture Elisha. He sent an army with horses and chariots to Dothan, where Elisha was staying. During the night, the army arrived and surrounded the city.

When Elisha's attendant rose early the next morning, he began to panic when he saw the Syrian army.

> *"Alas, my master! What shall we do?" He said, "Do not be afraid, for those who are with us are more than those who are with them." Then Elisha prayed and said, "O Lord, please open his eyes that he may see." So the Lord opened the eyes of the young man, and he saw, and behold, the mountain was full of horses and chariots of fire all around Elisha.*
>
> *2 Kings 6:15–17 ESV*

Elisha could see in the supernatural realm. He didn't see the enemy surrounding him. He saw that his enemy was far outnumbered and had no chance. Seeing with your spirit through the eyes of faith will keep you from surrendering to an outnumbered, defeated enemy.

It was important for Elisha's servant to see the same supernatural advantage that Elisha did. Likewise, Elijah's servant needed to see that the rain cloud, God's supernatural provision, was already on the way. When we, by faith, see what God is doing in the spiritual realm, it empowers us to claim the victory that already belongs to us.

Let Me Show You the Stars

God promised to make Abraham a great nation. At the age of seventy-five, we find in Genesis 12 the call of Abram (he would later be called Abraham), where God promises him the possession of land, numerous descendants, and blessings so great that the blessing would go beyond just his life and bless his entire lineage to follow. God made this promise to a childless man.

God asked Abram to leave his family's land and go to the land God would show him. Leaving his father's house meant abandoning his security and identity entirely. Abram's obedience required trusting God with his survival and his future.

He left everything he knew behind to follow God's instructions without knowing all the pieces of the puzzle. Though old, he didn't let his customs and routine keep him in the familiar. Vision will call you to what you've never known or experienced.

From the moment God called Abram, his life was built on vision. God met Abram in his obedience and showed him what to have faith in.

> *The LORD said to Abram, after Lot had separated from him, "Lift up your eyes and look from the place where you are, northward and southward and eastward and westward, for all the land that you see I will give to you and to your offspring forever. I will make your offspring as the dust of the earth, so that if one can count the dust of the earth, your offspring also can be counted. Arise, walk through the length and the breadth of the land, for I will give it to you."*
>
> *Genesis 13:14–17 ESV*

God caused Abram to be very wealthy with livestock, silver, and gold (Genesis 13:2). Part of God's promises were fulfilled, but he had yet to have a child. Imagine being Abram and all the years passing, holding to the vision—holding one part of the promise but not the other.

In Genesis 15, Abram expressed his frustration, asking if his servant, Eliezer, would be the heir to all his blessings because he still remained childless. God replied by again reaffirming his promise.

> *And behold, the word of the LORD came to him: "This man shall not be your heir;*

your very own son shall be your heir." And
he brought him outside and said, "Look
toward heaven, and number the stars,
if you are able to number them." Then he
said to him, "So shall your offspring be."
And he believed the Lord, *and he counted*
it to him as righteousness.

Genesis 15:4–6 ESV

God brought him outside and showed him the stars.
The life of Abraham teaches me that God doesn't want to
only tell me his promises; he wants to show them to me.
The more I obey, the more he gives me to see.

Reading this passage of Scripture, perhaps you envision a dark, starry night as I once did. Maybe you imagine Abram gazing up into a clear view of the Milky Way.
And while God can certainly give you a vision any way
he chooses, spiritual eyesight will most often be required.

As the chapter continues, God gets ready to make a
covenant with Abram. Notice what the Bible records a
few verses later.

As the sun was going down, a deep sleep
fell on Abram. And behold, dreadful and
great darkness fell upon him.

Genesis 15:12 ESV

"As the sun was going down." This description tells us that it wasn't even dark when God asked Abram to count the stars. Any middle school science class will teach you that just because you can't see the stars during the day doesn't mean they aren't there. There just isn't enough contrasting light to recognize them.

Abram had to look up into the sky and know that even though he could not see them with his natural eyes to count, the stars would soon appear. He may not have had children to count yet in the natural, but God was giving him a vision through the eyes of faith to see what already belonged to him.

What a powerful experience that must have been for Abram, seeing God once again confirm his promises are true. He must have felt such peace after that kind of supernatural confirmation. *But not everyone saw the stars that day.*

His wife Sarai wasn't out there with Abram looking at the stars together, yet she played a vital role in the outcome. She was to conceive this miracle baby but wasn't the one to see this vision firsthand. She not only had to trust God, but she also had to trust her husband.

Leadership will see things you didn't see firsthand. When I own the vision, it's my job to imagine it until I see it. I don't want my leadership to be looking at one thing ahead while I am looking in the opposite direction.

No, I need to see what my leadership sees. I need to see the vision with my spirit.

Confession Precedes Possession

What you see in the spirit realm will affect your actions. It will give weight to your confession. In Mark 11, Jesus tells his disciples:

> *Have faith in God. Truly, I say to you, whoever says to this mountain, "Be taken up and thrown into the sea," and does not doubt in his heart, but believes that what he says will come to pass, it will be done for him.*
>
> *Mark 11:22–23 ESV*

If you see with eyes of faith and never speak it, it will simply be a story of something you once saw. Our faith is put into action and becomes our reality through the confession of our words.

In his book *The Spirit of Faith*, Pastor Mark Hankins teaches how your voice is your address in the spirit. Scientists have proven that your voiceprint is just as accurate in identifying you as your fingerprint.[3]

While voices may sound similar on the surface, like

a fingerprint, endless variations exist. Structure, pitch, tone, rhythm, and frequency patterns are all examined when creating a digital profile of the voice.[4] These voice-prints are often used for security purposes and can provide high-level clearance and access. It proves you are who you say you are.

There is no voice like yours and, therefore, no confession like yours. Acting in faith is not the sole responsibility of leadership. Your voice of faith matters, too. What you think, see, and say will affect your true ownership of the vision.

Faith is always moving forward and never stands still. There will be crucial opportunities to operate skillfully in the spirit of faith. These will be your "get on" or "get off" the train moments. It's always a choice not to look at what you see in the natural but only what you see in the spirit.

What are you believing for? What is God calling you to accomplish? What is your vision? Can you hear it? Do you see it? Are you speaking it? Remember, confession always precedes possession.

It's time to take ownership of what God has called you to accomplish—ownership so deep that it becomes who you are. Advancement is yours. Increase belongs to you. Time is short, and there is much work to do.

So He May Run Who Reads It

In Habakkuk, we find a profound instruction that God gave the prophet.

> *Then the LORD answered me and said: "Write the vision and make it plain on tablets, that he may run who reads it. For the vision is yet for an appointed time; but at the end it will speak, and it will not lie. Though it tarries, wait for it; because it will surely come, it will not tarry."*
> *Habakkuk 2:2–3 NKJV*

When a vision is clear, it transforms from a message into a movement. Once seen, it cannot be ignored. It ignites in us a drive and urgency to live it out fully and to inspire others to do the same.

Even if you don't know how to accomplish it in the natural, you know that God is always true to his Word. We know the vision will come to pass when we faithfully obey his instructions.

It's time to become invaluable to your mission, and be the kind of team member that others can rely on to carry the vision forward with unwavering dedication. *Someone who will run after it with supernatural strength.*

Taking ownership of the vision goes beyond fulfilling a role or a simple job description. It is choosing to be someone who brings irreplaceable value. Those who own the vision are the loyal heartbeat, the immovable force, who bring passion, resilience, and a deep commitment that others can't help but notice.

This book is a call to pursue your vision with relentless dedication. It's about making yourself integral and indispensable, contributing in ways that bring lasting impact, and refusing to operate in anything less than excellence.

Just as God told Habakkuk to "write" the vision, making it clear and visible, we are to be living testimonies of our purpose. When we embody the vision deeply, it will radiate from our actions, decisions, and commitment.

When the vision becomes who we are, it doesn't sit untold on paper or remain confined within; it becomes a force that propels us forward, inviting others to follow. You are not just part of the vision—you are the vision. And as a result, the world will never be the same.

ACKNOWLEDGMENTS

Thank you, Lord.

Thank you, Mom,
for always being my greatest support.

Thank you Pastors Ted & Carolyn,
for everything.

NOTES

INTRODUCTION

1. Godin, Seth. *Linchpin: Are You Indispensable?* Portfolio, 2010.

2. Ibid.

THE GREAT PURSUIT

1. Sumrall, Lester. *Run with the Vision.* LeSEA Publishing, 1986.

2. Sumrall, Lester, and Tim Dudley. *The Life Story of Lester Sumrall.* New Leaf Press, 2003.

3. "Lester Sumrall Biography." *Feed The Hungry*, www.feedthehungry.org/lester-sum rall-biography. Accessed 11 Nov. 2024.

4. Sumrall, Lester, and Tim Dudley. *The Life Story of Lester Sumrall.* New Leaf Press, 2003.

5. Ibid.

6. "Impact." *Feed The Hungry*, www.feedthehungry.org/impact. Accessed 11 Nov. 2024.

7. New English Translation textual criticism note on Proverbs 29:18.

8. "William Tyndale." *Christianity Today,* 30 July 2019, www.christianitytoday.com/history/people/scholarsandscientists/william-tyndale.html.

9. Ibid.

10. "William Tyndale, England, Scholar." *365 Christian Men*, 2020, www.365christian men.com/podcast/william-tyndale-england-scholar/.

11. "William Tyndale: Did You Know?" *Christianity Today*, 30 July 2019, www.christi anitytoday.com/history/issues/issue-16/william-tyndale-did-you-know.html.

12. "William Tyndale, England, Scholar." *365 Christian Men*, 2020, www.365christian men.com/podcast/william-tyndale-england-scholar/.

13. "William Tyndale." *Christianity Today*, 30 July 2019, www.christianitytoday.com/history/people/scholarsandscientists/william-tyndale.html.

14. Oyedepo, David. *Vision: A Legacy Publication.* Dominion Publishing House, 2021.

TAKING OWNERSHIP

1. Williams, Serena, and Daniel Paisner. *On the Line.* Grand Central Publishing, 2009.

2. Ibid.

3.   Jiwani, Rory. *Serena Williams – Tennis Career Statistics and Facts*, olympics.com/en/ news/tennis-serena-williams-career-statistics-facts. Accessed 28 Sept. 2024.

4.   Sinek, Simon. *Start with Why: How Great Leaders Inspire Everyone to Take Action.* Portfolio, 2009.

5.   Ziglar, Zig. *Goals: How to Get the Most Out of Your Life.* Thomas Nelson, 2009

THE POSITION OF YOUR HEART

1.   McKane, William. *Proverbs: A New Approach.* Westminster Press, 1970. The Old Testament Library.

2.   "Google Dictionary (English)." *Oxford Languages,* Oxford University Press, www. languages.oup.com/google-dictionary-en/.

3.   Chapman, Gary. *The 5 Love Languages: The Secret to Love That Lasts.* Northfield Publishing, 1992.

4.   Hankins, Mark. *Honor: Above and Beyond.* Mark Hankins Ministries, 2022.

WITHOUT LIMIT

1.   Prince, Joseph. "The Mind of Christ Doesn't Grow Old." *Cfaith,* https://www. cfaith.com/the-mind-of-christ-doesnt-grow-old/. Accessed 25 Nov. 2024.

2.   Forleo, Marie. *Everything is Figureoutable.* Portfolio, 2019.

SELF-MANAGEMENT

1.   Vance, Ashlee. *Elon Musk: Tesla, Spacex, and the Quest for a Fantastic Future.* Ecco, an Imprint of HarperCollins Publishers, 2017.

2.   Ibid.

3.   "Everything Elon Musk Owns." *Madison Trust,* www.madisontrust.com/informa tion-center/visualizations/everything-elon-musk-owns/. Accessed 11 Nov. 2024.

4.   "Mission." *SpaceX,* www.spacex.com/mission/. Accessed 11 Nov. 2024.

5.   "What Real Discipline Looks Like." *Entrepreneur,* 28 Aug. 2016, www.entrepre neur.com/en-ae/growth-strategies/what-real-discipline-looks-like/281542.

6.   "Elon Musk's Productivity Hack: Taking Control of Your Schedule." *Yahoo! Tech,* 17 May 2023, www.yahoo.com/tech/elon-musks-productivity-hack-taing-093435057. html.

7.   "Elon Musk's $44B Twitter Deal by the Numbers." *S&P Global Market Intelligence,* 6 May 2022, www.spglobal.com/market-intelligence/en/news-insights/research/ elon-musks-44b-twitter-deal-by-the-numbers.

8.   "Time-Honoured: The In-Depth History of Rolex." *Wynn and Thayne,* 12 Dec. 2022, www.wynnandthayne.com/blogs/news/time-honoured-the-in-depth-histo ry-of-rolex.

9.   Keller, Gary, and Jay Papasan. *The ONE Thing: The Surprisingly Simple Truth Behind Extraordinary Results.* Bard Press, 2013.

TIME MANAGEMENT

1.   Sivers, Derek. "Where to Find the Hours to Make It Happen." *Sivers.org*, 1 Oct. 2019, https://sive.rs/uncomf.

2.   Dicks, Matthew. *Someday Is Today: 22 Simple, Actionable Ways to Propel Your Creative Life.* New World Library, 2022.

3.   Levitin, Daniel J. *The Organized Mind: Thinking Straight in the Age of Information Overload.* Dutton, 2014.

4.   Ibid.

5.   Kwik, Jim. *Limitless: Upgrade Your Brain, Learn Anything Faster, and Unlock Your Exceptional Life.* Hay House, 2020.

6.   Ibid.

7.   Timeular. "Eat the Frog: How to Overcome Procrastination and Get Things Done." *Timeular*, www.timeular.com/blog/eat-frog. Accessed 11 Nov. 2024.

BE A PROBLEM SOLVER

1.   Kwik, Jim. *Limitless: Upgrade Your Brain, Learn Anything Faster, and Unlock Your Exceptional Life.* Hay House, 2020.

2.   "Number of Possible Chess Games." *Enthu*, www.enthu.com/blog/chess/number-of-possible-chess-games/. Accessed 11 Nov. 2024.

3.   "Which Is Greater: Number of Atoms in the Universe or Number of Chess Moves?" *National Museums Liverpool*, www.liverpoolmuseums.org.uk/stories/which-greater-number-of-atoms-universe-or-number-of-chess-moves. Accessed 11 Nov. 2024.

4.   Bartlett, Steven. *The Diary of a CEO: The 33 Laws of Business and Life.* Penguin Publishing Group, 2023.

TAKE RESPONSIBILITY

1.   Willink, Jocko, and Leif Babin. *Extreme Ownership: How U.S. Navy SEALs Lead and Win.* St. Martin's Press, 2015.

2.   Duplantis, Jesse. *The Everyday Visionary: Focus Your Thoughts, Change Your Life.* Touchstone, 2008.

EFFECTIVE COMMUNICATION

1.   "Kermit Tyler: The Call That Would Live in Infamy." *The National WWII Museum*, 31 Oct. 2021, www.nationalww2museum.org/war/articles/kermit-tyler-call-would-live-infamy.

2.   Prange, Gordon W. *At Dawn We Slept: The Untold Story of Pearl Harbor.* Penguin Books, 1981.

3.   Frank, Richard B. "The Three Missed Tactical Warnings That Could Have Made a Difference at Pearl Harbor." *The National WWII Museum*, 13 Oct. 2021, www.nationalww2museum.org/war/articles/pearl-harbor-missed-tactical-warnings.

4. Prange, Gordon W. *At Dawn We Slept: The Untold Story of Pearl Harbor.* Penguin Books, 1981.

5. Frank, Richard B. "The Three Missed Tactical Warnings That Could Have Made a Difference at Pearl Harbor." *The National WWII Museum,* 13 Oct. 2021, www.nationalww2museum.org/war/articles/pearl-harbor-missed-tactical-warnings.

6. "Kermit Tyler: The Call That Would Live in Infamy." *The National WWII Museum,* 31 Oct. 2021, www.nationalww2museum.org/war/articles/kermit-tyler-call-would-live-infamy.

7. Prange, Gordon W. *At Dawn We Slept: The Untold Story of Pearl Harbor.* Penguin Books, 1981.

8. Whyte, William H. "Is Anybody Listening?" *Fortune,* vol. 42, no. 3, Time Inc., Sept. 1950, pp. 77, 174.

THE POWER OF SYSTEMS

1. "Henry Ford (1863)." *Energy Kids,* U.S. Energy Information Administration, www.eia.gov/kids/history-of-energy/famous-people/ford.php. Accessed 11 Nov. 2024.

2. "Model T." *Detroit Historical Society,* www.detroithistorical.org/learn/encyclopedia-of-detroit/model-t. Accessed 11 Nov. 2024.

3. Goss, Jennifer L. "Henry Ford and the Auto Assembly Line." *ThoughtCo,* 22 Jan. 2020, www.thoughtco.com/henry-ford-and-the-assembly-line-1779201.

4. "Ford's Assembly Line Starts Rolling." *History,* A&E Television Networks, 30 Nov. 2020, www.history.com/this-day-in-history/fords-assembly-line-starts-rolling.

5. Ibid.

6. Ibid.

7. "Edsel and Henry Ford with the Fifteen-Millionth Model T." *The Henry Ford,* www.thehenryford.org/collections-and-research/digital-collections/artifact/280343/. Accessed 11 Nov. 2024.

8. Klein, Christopher. "How McDonald's Beat Its Early Competition and Became an Icon of Fast Food." *History,* A&E Television Networks, 27 Sept. 2023, www.history.com/news/how-mcdonalds-became-fast-food-giant.

9. Plant, Porter. "What Does Henry Ford, McDonald's, and Your Content Have in Common?" *Medium,* 6 Dec. 2016, www.medium.com/everydaymarketers/what-does-heny-ford-mcdonalds-and-your-content-have-in-common-fda8a36b4eea.

10. Forte, Tiago. *Building a Second Brain: A Proven Method to Organize Your Digital Life and Unlock Your Creative Potential.* Atria Books, 2022.

FLEXIBILITY

1. Buffett, Warren, and Richard J. Connors. *Warren Buffett on Business: Principles from the Sage of Omaha.* Wiley, 2009.

2. Clear, James. *Atomic Habits: An Easy & Proven Way to Build Good Habits & Break Bad Ones.* Avery, 2018.

LOYALTY & HONOR

1. Giles, Rosemary. "Desmond Doss Was the Only Conscientious Objector to Receive the Medal of Honor in World War II." *War History Online*, 30 June 2023, www.warhistoryonline.com/world-war-ii/desmond-doss.html.

2. "Private First Class Desmond Thomas Doss Medal of Honor." *The National WWII Museum*, 12 Oct. 2020, www.nationalww2museum.org/war/articles/private-first-class-desmond-thomas-doss-medal-of-honor.

3. Ibid.

4. Lange, Katie. "Pfc. Desmond Doss: The Unlikely Hero Behind 'Hacksaw Ridge'." *The United States Army*, 28 Feb. 2017, www.army.mil/article/183328/pfc_desmond_doss_the_unlikely_hero_behind_hacksaw_ridge.

5. "Private First Class Desmond Thomas Doss Medal of Honor." *The National WWII Museum*, 12 Oct. 2020, www.nationalww2museum.org/war/articles/private-first-class-desmond-thomas-doss-medal-of-honor.

6. Lange, Katie. "Pfc. Desmond Doss: The Unlikely Hero Behind 'Hacksaw Ridge'." *The United States Army*, 28 Feb. 2017, www.army.mil/article/183328/pfc_desmond_doss_the_unlikely_hero_behind_hacksaw_ridge.

7. "Private First Class Desmond Thomas Doss Medal of Honor." *The National WWII Museum*, 12 Oct. 2020, www.nationalww2museum.org/war/articles/private-first-class-desmond-thomas-doss-medal-of-honor.

8. Lange, Katie. "Pfc. Desmond Doss: The Unlikely Hero Behind 'Hacksaw Ridge'." *The United States Army*, 28 Feb. 2017, www.army.mil/article/183328/pfc_desmond_doss_the_unlikely_hero_behind_hacksaw_ridge.

9. "Private First Class Desmond Thomas Doss Medal of Honor." *The National WWII Museum*, 12 Oct. 2020, www.nationalww2museum.org/war/articles/private-first-class-desmond-thomas-doss-medal-of-honor.

10. Lange, Katie. "Pfc. Desmond Doss: The Unlikely Hero Behind 'Hacksaw Ridge'." *The United States Army*, 28 Feb. 2017, www.army.mil/article/183328/pfc_desmond_doss_the_unlikely_hero_behind_hacksaw_ridge.

11. Ibid.

12. Hankins, Mark. *Honor: Above and Beyond*. Mark Hankins Ministries, 2022.

13. New English Translation textual criticism note on Exodus 20:12.

14. "G5091 / timao / – New Testament Greek." *Equip God's People*, www.equipgodspeople.com/lexicons-word-study/new-testament-greek/strongs-g5091.

SEEING THROUGH THE EYES OF FAITH

1. Bonnke, Reinhard. *Living a Life of Fire: An Autobiography*. E-R Productions, 2009.

2. Oyedepo, David. *The Unlimited Power of Faith*. Dominion Publishing House, 2011.

3. Hankins, Mark. *The Spirit of Faith*. Mark Hankins Ministries, 2012.

4. "Voice Identification." *Argus TrueID*, www.argustrueid.com/voice-identification/. Accessed 11 Nov. 2024.

BEFORE YOU GO

If you enjoyed this book, will you take a few minutes to leave a review on Amazon? This helps other potential readers to find and love it too. Thank you!

ABOUT THE AUTHOR

Tiffany Farley is a part of Miracle Word Ministries, under the leadership of Pastors Ted and Carolyn Shuttlesworth. She currently works in several ministry departments including media, production, marketing, administration, and publishing.

She is a graduate of Zion Bible Institute and currently resides in South Florida.